D1580496

059842
THE HENLEY COLLEGE LIBRARY

X-FORCE
YOU GOTTA BE KIDDIN'-?!
PHALANX COVENANT

X-FORCE

WRITERS
SCOTT LOBDELL, TODD DEZAGO
& FABIAN NICIEZA

PENCILERS
JAN DUURSEMA, ROGER CRUZ,
TONY DANIEL, KEN LASHLEY,
STEVE EPTING & TERRY DODSON

INKERS
AL MILGROM & KEVIN CONRAD WITH
PHILIP MOY, W.C. CARANI, JOHN FLOYD,
HARRY CANDELARIO, JOHN LIVESAY
& TIM TOWNSEND

COLORISTS
GLYNIS OLIVER, MARIE JAVINS,
CHRIS MATTHYS & MIKE THOMAS

LETTERERS
RICHARD STARKINGS & COMICRAFT,
CHRIS ELIOPOULOS & DAVE SHARPE
WITH BILL OAKLEY & PAT BROSSEAU

ASSISTANT EDITORS
JAYE GARDNER & BEN RAAB

EDITORS
KELLY CORVESE, BOB HARRAS
& SUZANNE GAFFNEY

COVER ARTISTS
TONY DANIEL, KEVIN CONRAD
& THOMAS MASON

VARIANT COVER ARTISTS
TONY DANIEL & KEVIN CONRAD

COLLECTION EDITOR
MARK D. BEAZLEY

ASSISTANT EDITORS
NELSON RIBEIRO & ALEX STARBUCK

EDITOR, SPECIAL PROJECTS
JENNIFER GRÜNWALD

SENIOR EDITOR, SPECIAL PROJECTS
JEFF YOUNGQUIST

RESEARCH & LAYOUT
JEPH YORK

PRODUCTION
COLORTEK & JOE FRONTIRRE

SVP OF PRINT & DIGITAL PUBLISHING SALES
DAVID GABRIEL

EDITOR IN CHIEF
AXEL ALONSO

CHIEF CREATIVE OFFICER
JOE QUESADA

PUBLISHER
DAN BUCKLEY

EXECUTIVE PRODUCER
ALAN FINE

PHALANX COVENANT

-FORCE: PHALANX COVENANT. Contains material originally published in magazine form as X-FACTOR #106, X-FORCE #38-43 and EXCALIBUR #82. First printing 2013. ISBN# 978-0-
351-6271-1. Published by MARVEL WORLDWIDE, INC., a subsidiary of MARVEL ENTERTAINMENT, LLC. OFFICE OF PUBLICATION: 135 West 50th Street, New York, NY 10020. **Printed in China.** ALAN FINE, EVP - Office of the President, Marvel Worldwide, Inc. and EVP &
MO Marvel Characters B.V.; DAN BUCKLEY, Publisher & President - Print, Animation & Digital Divisions; JOE QUESADA, Chief Creative Officer; TOM BREVOORT, SVP of Publishing; DAVID
OGART, SVP of Operations & Procurement, Publishing; C.B. CEBULSKI, SVP of Creator & Content Development; DAVID GABRIEL, SVP of Print & Digital Publishing Sales; JIM O'KEEFE,
P of Operations & Logistics; DAN CARR, Executive Director of Publishing Technology; SUSAN CRESPI, Editorial Operations Manager; ALEX MORALES, Publishing Operations Manager;
TAN LEE, Chairman Emeritus. For information regarding advertising in Marvel Comics or on Marvel.com, please contact Niza Disla, Director of Marvel Partnerships, at ndisla@marvel.
om. For Marvel subscription inquiries, please call 800-217-9158. **Manufactured between 4/22/2013 and 6/17/2013 by R.R. DONNELLEY ASIA PRINTING SOLUTIONS, CHINA.**

0 9 8 7 6 5 4 3 2 1

MARVEL COMICS
X-FACTOR
$2.95 US
$4.00 CAN/£2.00 UK
106
SEP
02145
APPROVED BY THE COMICS CODE AUTHORITY
X-MEN
EVENT
PHALANX COVENANT
LIFE SIGNS
PART 1

The Phalanx have emerged. A shapeshifting, techno-organic, matter-assimilating race of creatures derived from the deceased alien New Mutants member named Warlock, and directed by anti-mutant bigots Stephen Lang and Cameron Hodge, the Phalanx have targeted the X-Men — and all of mutantkind — for extinction.

Phalanx units battled Rogue, Archangel, Storm, Gambit and the X-Men's ally Yukio, but all were defeated. Meanwhile, a Phalanx unit modeled on Warlock and his fellow deceased New Mutants teammate, Doug Ramsey, somehow achieved independence. Summoned by Zero, the teleporting android formerly used by the MLF's Stryfe, "Douglock" defected from the Phalanx collective and aided Zero against Stryfe's hunter-killer robots. Excalibur became involved in the battle, and although Shadowcat was initially confused and angry at the Phalanx unit in the form of her dead friend, Douglock eventually chose to remain with Excalibur.

The Phalanx soon realized that mutants were immune to absorption by the alien techno-virus that spawned their race. Determined to overcome this immunity, they captured the X-Men and experimented on them. The Phalanx replaced the mutants with disguised drones, but retired X-Man Banshee eventually saw through the ruse. Gathering Emma Frost, Jubilee and the captive Sabretooth into an ad hoc team, Banshee destroyed the drones and detonated Cerebro, which the Phalanx were using to locate more mutants for study. Banshee's group then tracked down the neo-mutants already captured by the Phalanx, including Cannonball's younger sister Paige Guthrie, and rescued them — though the young woman known as Blink inadvertently sacrificed herself to defeat the Phalanx holding them captive.

Meanwhile, acting on Professor X's psychic summons, Cable, Wolverine and newlyweds Cyclops and Phoenix converged on Muir Island, which had become infested with Phalanx. The four mutants battled through the techno-organic creatures and accessed Muir Island's backup Cerebro unit, using it to learn that the X-Men were being held captive in the Himalayas. After defeating Muir Island's Phalanx, the group made their way to the creatures' Himalayan base, assaulted it and freed the X-Men, destroying the base in the process.

Though both Banshee's team and the X-Men were able to eliminate the Phalanx units they fought, the other X-teams — X-Force, X-Factor and Excalibur — have a far more difficult task. With Douglock's aid, they must prevent the Phalanx from contacting the alien race that spawned them, and summoning them to Earth…

IT IS A COLD, RELENTLESS RAIN THAT BATTERS DOWN UPON THE CENTURIES-OLD STRUCTURE THAT IS THE MONT SAINT FRANCIS --
-- AN ABANDONED FRANCISCAN MONASTERY SITUATED ALONG THE NORTHERN COAST OF FRANCE. *
SUDDENLY, A SPHERE COMPRISED SOLELY OF ELECTRO-MAGNETIC ENERGY DROPS FROM THE HEAVY, BLACK, LEADEN CLOUDS...
....ALL BUT INVISIBLE, SAVE FOR ITS OUTLINE, DELINEATED BY THE POUNDING RAIN, AND ITS RATHER DYNAMIC PASSENGERS --
*LAST SEEN IN UNCANNY X-MEN #300 -- Kelly.
-- THE MUTANT TEAM KNOWN AS X-FACTOR --
-- THE SPHERE FLOATS GENTLY SHOREWARD...
I DUNNO, FORGE. ARE YOU SURE DISSIS DA PLACE?
LOOKS KIN'A DEAD T'ME.
PROFESSOR XAVIER'S MESSAGE WAS URGENT AND CRYPTIC, GUIDO.
HE GAVE ME THESE COORDINATES, TOLD US TO COME IMMEDIATELY.
BUT HE DEMANDED THAT WE NOT BRING ANY FORM OF TECHNOLOGY WHATSOEVER WITH US.
HE COULDN'T SAY MORE, BUT WHEN YOU HEAR EVEN A HINT OF FEAR IN THE VOICE OF A MAN LIKE CHARLES XAVIER --
-- WELL, YOU FIND YOURSELF WONDERING AT WHAT COULD DISTRESS A MAN LIKE HIM.
SNFF SNFF
WHAT'S THE MATTER, RAHNE...?
SOMETHIN' DOESNA SMELL RIGHT...
I CANNA GET A GOOD SCENT ON IT, WHAT WITH THE WET O' THE STORM, BUT --
ZZKAK

SORRY FOR THE FIREWORKS DISPLAY, X-FACTOR!
BUT YOU HAVETA STAY WHERE YA ARE UNTIL Y'ALL ARE DIRECTED TO DO OTHER-WISE.
I WILL APOLOGIZE IN ADVANCE IF OUR COLD RECEPTION PROVES TO HAVE BEEN UNNEEDED, MEIN FREUNDS ...
...BUT CONSIDERING WHAT WE HAVE RECENTLY EXPERIENCED, WE CAN AFFORD TO TAKE NO CHANCES.
NIGHT-CRAWLER, WHAT "CHANCES" ARE YOU TALKING ABOUT?
AND WHAT IS EXCALIBUR AND X-FORCE DOING HERE?
WHAT EXACTLY IS GOING ON?
AGAIN, I AM SORRY, FORGE, BUT WITH THE CIRCUMSTANCES BEING WHAT THEY ARE --
-- UNTIL WE'RE ABLE TO PROVE YOUR AUTHENTICITY, I'M AFRAID THAT WE CAN'T ALLOW YOU TO PROCEED ANY FARTHER.
"AUTHENTICITY"...?
WOULD SOMEONE JUS' SPEAK PLAIN ENGLISH AROUND HERE?
SAM, PLEASE, WE KNOW SOMETHING'S DREADFULLY WRONG...OR ELSE THE PROFESSOR WOULDNA' HAVE GATHERED US ALL.
BUT, HOW CAN YE NOT KNOW 'TIS ME?
I'M SORRY, RAHNE... BUT UNTIL WE KNOW FOR SURE, WE CAN'T DEPEND ON TRUST ALONE.

ARE YOU KIDDIN' ME...?
WE CAME ALL DIS WAY, JUS' T'STAND IN THE RAIN AN' GET TREATED LIKE A BUNCHA SECOND CLASS CITIZENS...?
I DON'T THINK SO.
GUIDO, BACK OFF... NOW!
DON'T PUSH THIS, GUIDO!
Oh, I'M SCARED. WHADDAYA GONNA DO?
CHILL OUT CANNON BALL. YOU BEEN WATCHIN' TOO MANY "TERMINATOR" MOVIES.
BOOM
WHOA.
THAT WUZ BOOMER PROTECTIN' SAMMY, WUZN'T IT?
GUIDO, CALM DOWN!
SORRY, 'LEX, BUT I T'INK BOOMER JUS' ASKED ME ONNA DATE --
-- AN' I WOULD HATE T'DENY HER MY EBULLIENT PERSONALITY!
IT WOULD SEEM CAUTIOUSNESS IS NOT STRONG GUY'S STRONG SUIT.
BAMF
DON'T TAUNT HIM, KURT, JUST HOLD HIM!
C'MON, YA BIG STEROID-ENRICHED APE! I'M READY FOR YA!
ENOUGH!

STAN LEE presents:
the Phalanx Covenant
LIFE SIGNS
PART 1
plot: SCOTT LOBDELL TODD DeZAGO
script: TODD DeZAGO
pencils: JAN DUURSEMA ROGER CRUZ
inks: AL MILGROM
letters: STARKINGS/ COMICRAFT
colors: GLYNIS OLIVER
cover: STEVE LIGHTLE
editor: KELLY CORVESE
group editor: BOB HARRAS
chief: TOM DeFALCO
THIS JUVENILE BEHAVIOR MUST CEASE! WE'VE NEITHER THE TIME NOR THE ENERGY TO WASTE ON SENSELESS BRAWLS AMONGST OURSELVES.
MY APOLOGIES, X-FACTOR, FOR THE LESS-THAN-WARM WELCOME YOU RECEIVED UPON YOUR ARRIVAL.
IN LIGHT OF WHAT HAS OCCURRED OVER THE LAST TWENTY-FOUR HOURS IT WAS NECESSARY THAT WE ADOPT A "DOUBT FIRST, ASK QUESTIONS LATER" POLICY.
NOW THAT I HAVE HAD THE OPPORTUNITY TO TELEPATHICALLY SCAN YOU TO DETERMINE YOUR... AS KURT SO DELICATELY PUT IT... "AUTHENTICITY"...
...I WOULD LIKE TO THANK YOU AND SAY HOW GRATEFUL I AM THAT YOU CAME SO QUICKLY.
REST ASSURED THAT I WOULD NOT HAVE ASKED YOU TO MAKE SUCH A PERILOUS JOURNEY...
...HAD IT NOT BEEN VERY MUCH A MATTER OF LIFE AND DEATH!

WAIT, PROFESSOR! X-FACTOR HONORED YOUR "NO TECHNOLOGY" ORDER IN COMING HERE! BUT WHAT OF FORGE WITH HIS CYBERNETIC HAND AND LEG?
WHY IS HE THE EXCEPTION?
YOU SOUND SUSPICIOUS, SHATTER-STAR.
IF WE ARE TO SURVIVE THE COMING THREAT,
WE WILL HAVE TO DEPEND ON ONE ANOTHER, BODY AND SOUL.
I HAVE CLEARED FORGE, THAT SHOULD BE ENOUGH.
GOT THAT, SONNY BOY?
I MEANT NO DISRESPECT, ONLY CAUTION.
AW, C'MON, SAM. I WUZ JUST PLAYIN' AROUN'... I DIN'T MEAN ANYTHIN' BY IT.
I'M LIKE A BIG KID, I'M JUS' HAVIN' SOME FUN WIT' YA...
YE BEST F'RGIVE 'IM, SAM. IF YE DON'T, HE'LL NEVER LEAVE YE BE.
CHARLES... WHAT'S GOING ON? WHERE'RE ORORO AND THE OTHERS?
HAS SOMETHING HAPPENED TO THE X-MEN?! TO ORORO?
TELL ME !?!
FORGE -- I'M AFRAID SOMETHING HAS HAPPENED AND I FEAR FOR THE X-MEN'S SAFETY.
BUT PERHAPS, WE SHOULD WAIT UNTIL WE GET INSIDE TO DISCUSS THINGS.
WAIT?! PROFESSOR -- THESE ARE OUR FRIENDS WE'RE TALKING ABOUT!
MINE AS WELL, ALEX.
NOW COME INSIDE AND I SHALL TELL YOU OF THE PHALANX!

ONCE INSIDE THE SANCTUARY...

AS NEAR AS I CAN TELL, WE'RE BEING **HUNTED**, BY WHAT I BELIEVE TO BE A TERRIFYING, TECHNO-ORGANIC LIFE FORM...

...ONE **EAGER** TO PROVE ITSELF THE DOMINANT SPECIES, SIMPLY BY ELIMINATING ALL OTHER LIFE ON THE PLANET.

THESE ENTITIES CALL THEMSELVES THE **PHALANX**, AND THEY CAN INCORPORATE BOTH LIVING AND NON-LIVING MATERIALS INTO THEIR MASS.

THEY ARE CAPABLE OF SHAPING THEMSELVES INTO **ANY** FORM, TO THE POINT OF ACTUALLY CREATING DUPLICATES OF PEOPLE.

AND I BELIEVE...

...I **FEAR**...

...THAT THEY HAVE CLAIMED **THE X-MEN** AS THEIR VICTIMS.

"OUR LAST CONTACT WITH THE X-MEN WAS LESS THAN TWENTY-FOUR HOURS AGO, AS NIGHTCRAWLER RAN A DATA TRANSFERRAL PROGRAM IN THE RECORDS ROOM AT MUIR ISLAND.

"THE **BEAST** WAS HIS CONTACT AT THE MANSION. *

...HANK, YOU SEEM DISTRACTED -- ARE YOU ALL RIGHT?

CERTAINLY.

* IT WASN'T BEAST AT ALL, BUT A PHALANX-CLONE. SEE UNCANNY X-MEN #316. --Kelly

HOLD THE PHONE, NIGHT-CRAWLER.
THERE SEEMS TO BE SOME SORT OF DISTURBANCE IN THE READY ROOM.

BE BACK IN A SECOND.

"HE WAS ONLY GONE FOR A MOMENT, WHEN...

SHOOM
"WE CAN ONLY ASSUME THE WORST, BASED ON WHAT HAPPENED HERE NEXT.

I SENSE SOMETHING... KURT, SHUT DOWN THAT CONSOLE! GET AWA-
Eh...?
"I HAD BEEN DRAWN TO THE RECORDS ROOM BY THE SUDDEN ARRIVAL OF A NEW CONSCIOUSNESS TO THE FACILITY...
"...AND WHILE ITS COLLECTIVE INTELLIGENCE MADE IT IMPOSSIBLE FOR ME TO EVEN APPROACH ITS THOUGHTS WITH MY MIND...
"...I HAD BEEN ABLE TO DISCERN THAT ITS INTENTIONS WERE DEADLY.
VAS IST...?
SUBJECT: DESIGNATE -- KURT WAGNER/ NIGHTCRAWLER -- XAVIER CHARLES --
MUTANT CANDIDATES FOR COLLECTIVE ASSIMILATION. FUNCTION ANALYSIS -- 110101 --
-- DETAIN/RESTRAIN FOR ASSIMILATION PROCESS.
"KURT EVADED THE PHALANX'S ATTEMPTS AT CAPTURE...
"...MAKING MY SAFETY HIS TOP PRIORITY.
"HOWEVER...
HOLD ON, PROFESSOR!
I'LL HAVE US OUT OF HERE IN A MOMENT.
NO, NIGHT-CRAWLER! WAIT--
BAMF
MEIN GOTT, PROFESSOR! WHAT WERE THOSE --

...HORRORS?
BAMF
MY APOLOGIES, KURT, FOR TELEPATHICALLY OVERRIDING YOUR POWER OF TELEPORTATION --
-- BUT I THINK IT BEST THAT I REMAIN HERE, KEEPING THESE MENACES OCCUPIED --
-- WHILE YOU AND MOIRA SHUT DOWN ALL POWER AND SECURE THE ENTIRE COMPLEX.
BUT, PROFESSOR --
YOUR CONCERN IS TOUCHING, KURT, BUT I'M NOT WITHOUT MY OWN RESOURCES.
BY KEEPING THESE CREATURES ON THE DEFENSE WITH SOME TELEPATHIC SUGGESTIONS...
...I CAN BUY YOU THE TIME NEEDED TO COMPLETE YOUR GOAL.
I ASSURE YOU, I CAN HANDLE MYSELF.

BAMF
" -- NIGHTCRAWLER WAS GONE...
SSHUK
"...LEAVING ME TO LIVE UP TO MY OWN CONFIDENT WORDS --
" -- AS I WATCHED WITH A CERTAIN AMOUNT OF AWE --
"-- THE SEVERED AND BROKEN 'LIMBS' OF THE PHALANX --
"-- COAGULATE AND CONGEAL INTO A LARGER, MORE THREATENING ADVERSARY.
FUNCTION ANALYSIS: RESPONSE TO ONSLAUGHT HIGH-LEVEL TELEPATHIC FORCE -- 11000 --
-- 001011 -- ADJUSTMENT OF DIMENSIONAL PARAMETERS TO FACILITATE CAPTURE -- 0110.
"AT THIS POINT, I REALIZED THIS THREAT WAS EVEN GREATER THAN I HAD ANTICIPATED. I KNEW I WOULD NEED REINFORCEMENTS --
I'VE GOT IT, PROFESSOR!
-- 1011 -- 11100000 --
"SHADOWCAT PHASED, NOT ONLY THROUGH THE CEILING...
"...BUT THROUGH MY GIANT FOE AS WELL --
"-- HER POWER DISRUPTING ITS TECHNO-ORGANIC CIRCUITRY AND TEMPORARILY NEUTRALIZING IT AS A THREAT.
KURT TOLD ME YOU --

Huh?
KURT AND MOIRA WERE ABLE TO SHUT DOWN THE POWER AND SEAL THE FACILITY.
BUT AS I FEARED, IT HAS NOT DONE MUCH TO HINDER THEIR ATTACK.
ALL WE HAVE MANAGED TO DO IS LOCK OURSELVES IN HERE WITH IT.
IT ALSO SEEMS THAT WHILE YOUR PHASING POWER IS THE MOST EFFECTIVE AGAINST THESE MONSTROSITIES...
...THERE ARE SOME ASPECTS OF THIS CREATURE THAT HAVEN'T GOTTEN THE MESSAGE!
WELL, I'LL BE MORE THAN HAPPY TO FIX THAT LITTLE "COMMUNICATION PROBLEM."
PROFESSOR, THE SIMILARITIES HERE WOULD BE JUST TOO COINICIDENTAL.
DO YOU THINK THERE'S A CONNECTION BETWEEN THESE BIO-TECHNIC CREATURES AND DOUGLOCK?
YES, KATHERINE, THERE IS, AS I WAS ORIGINALLY PART OF THIS COLLECTIVE INTELLIGENCE WHICH CALLS ITSELF THE PHALANX.
BUT THAT INFORMATION CAN WAIT. WE MUST FIRST ATTEND TO THE SITUATION BEFORE US.
I CANNOT PERMIT THE PHALANX TO ASSIMILATE THE TEAM MEMBERS OF EXCALIBUR.
YEAH, GOOD IDEA. LET'S NOT "PERMIT" THAT.
SKA-BASHH
HURRY! WE ARE EVACUATING THE ISLAND!
BRIAN! AMANDA!
THESE CREATURES ARE SPREADING THROUGHOUT THE COMPLEX AT AN INCREDIBLE RATE!

"INDEED IT HAD, WHICH WE SOON DISCOVERED WHILE TRYING TO LEAVE THE ISLAND IN THE TEAM'S HOVER-CRAFT...
ACH, IT'S GOT US! I'VE NO RESPONSE FROM THE CONTROLS!
FUNCTIONAL ANALYSIS: ABORT DEPARTURE OF CRAFT -- CAPTURE SUBJECTS DESIGNATE TEAM -- EXCALIBUR --
HOLD TIGHT, EVERYONE! WE MAY HAVE THE POWER TO BREAK FREE!!
"AS IT TURNS OUT, WE DID HAVE SUCH POWER, IN THE FORM OF BRITANIC...
"...WHOSE SHEER MIGHT WAS ENOUGH TO BREAK US FREE OF THE PHALANX'S GRASP.
KRA
KOOM
"WE BREATHED A COLLECTIVE SIGH OF RELIEF, AS WE CONTINUED OUR HASTY RETREAT!
"LESS THAN AN HOUR LATER WE APPROACHED OUR DESTINATION...
... AT MONT SAINT FRANCIS."

ONCE WE LAND, WE MUST FORMULATE A PLAN.
AT ALL COSTS, EXCALIBUR, WE MUST NOT ALLOW THE PHALANX AN OPPORTUNITY TO LEAVE MUIR.
THE BIOLOGICAL DATA THEY NOW HAVE AT THEIR DIS-- WHA--?!
1101010 -- CONFIRM APPREHENSION OF DESIGNATE XAVIER CHARLES -- 10101 --
"MY HOVERCHAIR HAD BEEN COMPROMISED. AS IT LOCKED ME IN IT'S DEADLY GRIP, PINNING ME TO IT...
"...WE CAME TO REALIZE THAT THE ENTIRE SHIP HAD BEEN INFESTED WITH IT, AS THE VERY WALLS SPRANG TO PHALANX-LIFE.
"ONLY MOMENTS BEFORE, I HAD STATED THE IMPORTANCE OF ISOLATING THE PHALANX ON MUIR ISLAND...
"...OF DENYING IT ANOTHER FOOTHOLD IN THE WORLD.
"WERE THE PHALANX ABLE TO ESTABLISH A BROAD ENOUGH BASE, IT COULD FEASIBLY WIPE OUT THE HUMAN RACE IN A MATTER OF WEEKS.
"I WOULD NOT BE RESPONSIBLE FOR THAT.
DESTRUC
"I BADE MOIRA TO INITIATE THE SHIP'S SELF-DESTRUCT PROGRAM.

"EVENTUALLY, WE MADE OUR WAY TO HERE."
SHAKA KOOOOMM
"AT THE LAST MINUTE, AMANDA CONSTRUCTED A MYSTICAL SPHERE TO SHIELD US FROM THE BLAST.
THIS MONASTERY WAS ONCE THE BASE OF OPERATIONS OF MAGNETO'S ACOLYTES...
DUE TO AN AS YET, UNEXPLAINED NATURAL PHENOMENON IT CONCEALS THE PRESENCE AND ACTIVITIES OF MUTANTS.
IRONICALLY, IT'S COME TO SERVE OUR PURPOSES, NOW...AS A SANCTUARY... AND A SAFE-HOUSE.
WE ARE GOING TO NEED EVERY ADVANTAGE WE CAN GET IN OUR BATTLE AGAINST THE PHALANX.
...THE STAKES ARE MUCH TOO HIGH FOR US NOT TO.

SO THIS, THEN, IS HOW YOU HANDLE THE GREATEST THREAT TO YOUR EXISTENCE... ?
BY TURNING TAIL AND RUNNING... !?!
LOOK, SHATTERSTAR, I'VE HAD ENOUGH OF YOUR CONDESCENDING ATTITUDE!
IF YOU WANT TO JUST BULL YOUR WAY THROUGH EVERY SITUATION --
SHATTERSTAR, THERE IS NO SHAME IN ACKNOWLEDGING YOUR OWN LIMITATIONS, OR DRAWING STRENGTH FROM ONE ANOTHER --
-- INDEED, THAT IS THE VERY REASON THAT I BROUGHT TOGETHER THE X-MEN IN THE FIRST PLACE.
SEEMS LIKE EVER'TIME SHATTERSTAR OPENS HIS MOUTH, AH'M THE ONE WHO GETS EMBAR-RASSED. HUH, RAHNE?
RAHNIE...?
UH-OH, GIRL. WHERE'D YOU GET OFF TO NOW?

"SO WE ARE TO GO THEN, AND RESCUE THE VAUNTED X-MEN?"
"NO, SHATTERSTAR. I HAVE ALREADY SET CABLE AND WOLVERINE TO THE TASK OF LOCATING THE X-MEN. *
* SEE CABLE #16 AND WOLVERINE #85 -- THE PHALANX COVENANT: FINAL SANCTION--Kelly.
"APPARENTLY, THE PHALANX HAVE SOME VESTED INTEREST IN MUTANTS. WHILE THEY HUNT US, BANSHEE HAS LEARNED THAT THEY HAVE ALSO TARGETED A COLLECTION OF NEO-MUTANTS.
"HE, ALONG WITH SEVERAL OTHERS, ARE WORKING TO PREVENT THEIR CAPTURE.
"NO, OURS MAY BE THE MOST DIFFICULT TASK OF ALL, THAT OF FINDING A WAY TO STOP THE PHALANX...
"...ALTHOUGH THE ANSWER TO THAT QUESTION MAY BE UNDER OUR VERY NOSES."
MEGGAN!?
I DINNA SENSE YE. YUIR SCENT HAS... CHANGED?
I HAVE CHANGED, RAHNE, SINCE LAST WE MET.
I AM MORE CERTAIN OF WHO I AM, OF MY PLACE IN THIS WORLD.
AND YET, I'M MUCH THE SAME.
I KNOW WHY YOU'VE COME DOWN HERE. YOUR WHOLE AURA RADIATES WITH LOVE AND HOPE...
...BUT YOU'RE TORN BY CONFUSION AND FEAR.
PLEASE, MEGGAN!
YE'VE GOT T'LET ME SEE 'IM!
SEEMS LIKE EVERY TIME WE TURN AROUND LATELY, WE'RE LOSIN' ONE O' OUR FRIENDS... OUR FAMILY.
BUT HEREIN GOD'S DECIDED THAT WE CAN HAVE DOUG BACK, AN' I JUST CANNAE WAIT ANY LONGER T'SEE 'IM.

THEN GO IN, RAHNE. I'M ONLY HERE TO KEEP AN EYE ON HIM.
I'M NOT KEEPING HIM IN... AND I'M NOT KEEPING ANY-ONE OUT.
YE MEAN I CAN...
GO AHEAD.
DOUG...?
IS IT REALLY YOU...?
Oh, SWEET HEAVEN...
--IT IS.
IT IS NOT.
AT LEAST, NOT THE DOUG RAMSEY THAT RAHNE SINCLAIR KNEW AS A FRIEND AND TEAMMATE DURING HER TIME WITH THE NEW MUTANTS.
NOT THE DOUG WHO HEROICALLY SACRIFICED HIS LIFE, SO LONG AGO, TO SAVE HERS.
AND WHILE SHE CAN SEE THIS WITH HER EYES, HER HEART TELLS HER OTHERWISE, AS EVERY FIBER OF HER BEING IS FILLED WITH JOY AT THE SIGHT OF HER LONG-LOST FRIEND.

ACH! 'TIS A MIRACLE!!
DOUG! Oh, HOW I'VE MISSED YE!
BUT, WHAT HAVE THEY DONE T'YE? THEY'VE GOT YE STRUNG UP LIKE SOME KIND O' CHRISTMAS TURKEY...
IT WAS MY SUGGESTION THAT I CONFINE AND RESTRAIN MYSELF TO THIS CHAMBER, UNTIL IT COULD BE DETERMINED TO THE SATISFACTION OF EVERYONE --
-- THAT I DO NOT PRESENT A THREAT TO THE CARBONITES.
WHY, THAT'S RIDICULOUS! WHAT POSSIBLE THREAT COULD YE POSE T'THE PEOPLE YE LO --
SAM!!
RAHNE!! WHAT THE HECK D'YA THINK YOU'RE DOIN', SNEAKIN' OFF LIKE THAT IN THE MIDDLE OF A BRIEFIN'...?
PROF SAYS THERE'S ONE O'THEM PHALANX-THINGS DOWN HERE, AN' IT MAY BE A LOT OF THINGS, BUT IT SURE AIN'T...
...DOUG?

YE *SEE*, SAM! YE KNOW 'TIS DOUG, AS WELL! I DINNA KEN HOW OR WHY, BUT HE'S *BACK*...
...AN' THAT'S ALL THAT MATTERS!
RAHNE, WAIT!
YOU ARE MISTAKEN, RAHNE SINCLAIR. I AM MERELY THE CEREBRAL AND GENETIC IMPRINT OF RAMSEY, DOUG --
-- AND DESIGNATE: WARLOCK, AS INTERPRETED BY THE PHALANX.
DINNA *TEASE* ME LIKE THIS, DOUG. THIS IS NOTHIN' T'JOKE ABOOT. 'TIS A VERY SERIOUS MATTER!
INDEED IT IS, RAHNE... *DEADLY* SERIOUS.
A MATTER SO SERIOUS THAT I'M AFRAID, TO GIVE OUR *TRUST* SO BLINDLY --
-- COULD VERY WELL GET US *ALL* KILLED.

SURELY YE CANNA MEAN THAT, PROFESSOR?
I DO, WHICH IS WHY I'VE ASKED FORGE HERE TO OFFER HIS OPINION.
PERHAPS HIS MUTANT POWER, HIS *INTUITIVE* ABILITY TO "SEE" HOW THINGS WORK, CAN HELP TO SHED SOME LIGHT ON --

-- FORGE?

ELSEWHERE IN EUROPE--
HIS NAME IS GIUSEPPE RUSSO, AND HE HAS BEEN A SHEPHERD FOR MOST ALL OF HIS SIXTY-EIGHT YEARS.
HE ENJOYS THE SOLITUDE OF HIS PASTORAL VOCATION.
HIS ENTIRE ADULT LIFE HAS BEEN DEVOTED TO THE TASK OF TENDING THE FLOCK.
INDEED, HE KNOWS THEM AS IF THEY WERE PEOPLE. WHEN THEY "SPOOK," IT IS USUALLY BECAUSE THEY HAVE CAUGHT WIND OF A NEARBY PREDATOR --
-- AN ERRANT WOLF OR BEAR THAT HAS WANDERED DOWN OUT OF THE MOUNTAINS...
COME, HUMAN, SHINAR HAS NEED OF YOU.
FOR THE MESSAGE MUST PASS THE STARS TO OUR PEOPLE!
WE HAVE FOUND A WORLD RIPE FOR CONQUEST!
HIS LAST THOUGHT IS THE QUESTION THAT HIS LIFE HAS ANSWERED...
WHO WILL TEND TO THE FLOCK?

WITHIN THE WOMB-LIKE CORE OF THE PHALANX'S COLLECTIVE INTELLIGENCE "RESIDES" THE BITTER REMAINS OF THE MAN WHO WAS STEPHEN LANG --
NOW, NOTHING MORE THAN A BLURRY MEMORY OF HUMANITY, HE FUNCTIONS AS THE HUMAN HOST OF THE INTELLIGENCE, OVER-SEEING A MYRIAD OF OPERATIONS --
-- EACH ONE DESIGNED TO BRING THE PHALANX EVER CLOSER TO THEIR OVERALL OBJECTIVE.
this is LUDICROUS!
SHINAR'S THOUGHTS, ARE BLOCKED TO ME
OF LATE, HOWEVER, HE HAS FOUND HIM-SELF REPEATEDLY CONFRONTED WITH --
independent thought!
there is no room in the collective for singular activities.
priority: analyze directive to purge independent operatives from collective.
SQUNCH
hodge!

hodge, it would seem that we are accessing more and more data involving phalanx agents operating of their own accord.
correct us if we're wrong, hodge, but wouldn't the designation "collective" intelligence preclude the concept of individual thought...?
one of them went so far as to assimilate a canine!
YOU AS WELL AS ANYONE SHOULD KNOW THAT ANY NEW PROGRAM HAS SOME KINKS TO WORK OUT.
SPLUT
THE PHALANX IS NOTHING IF NOT CONSTANTLY EVOLVING, ALWAYS ADAPTING TO AN INFINITE NUMBER OF POTENTIAL PROGRAMS.
THERE WILL ALWAYS BE UNFORSEEABLE... "GLITCHES."
FZZT
SNAK
FZZT
I MUST BE GETTING BACK NOW. WE ARE RUNNING EVERY CONCEIVABLE PROGRAM IN AN ATTEMPT TO ASCERTAIN WHY THE MUTANTS CANNOT BE ASSIMILATED INTO THE COLLECTIVE INTELLIGENCE.
SPLOOTCH
HODGE! you were not dismissed!
we demand to know how we are being overridden in this matter. we demand to know what is the cause for this increasing...
...rebelliousness.

MONT SAINT FRANCIS
IT IS THE MOST GENUINELY BEAUTIFUL SIGHT THAT THE MAN CALLED FORGE HAS SEEN IN HIS ENTIRE LIFE.
FROM THE DAY, AS AN ADOLESCENT, THAT HIS MUTANT POWER FIRST MANIFESTED ITSELF, HE HAS FELT ALONE, SET APART --
-- POSSESSING A VISION WHICH ENABLES HIM TO "SEE" AS NO OTHER MAN CAN SEE THE WORKINGS OF ALL THINGS MECHANICAL, TO UNDERSTAND HOW THEY OPERATE --
-- FROM THE SIMPLEST OF DEVICES --
--TO THE GREATEST OF MACHINES.

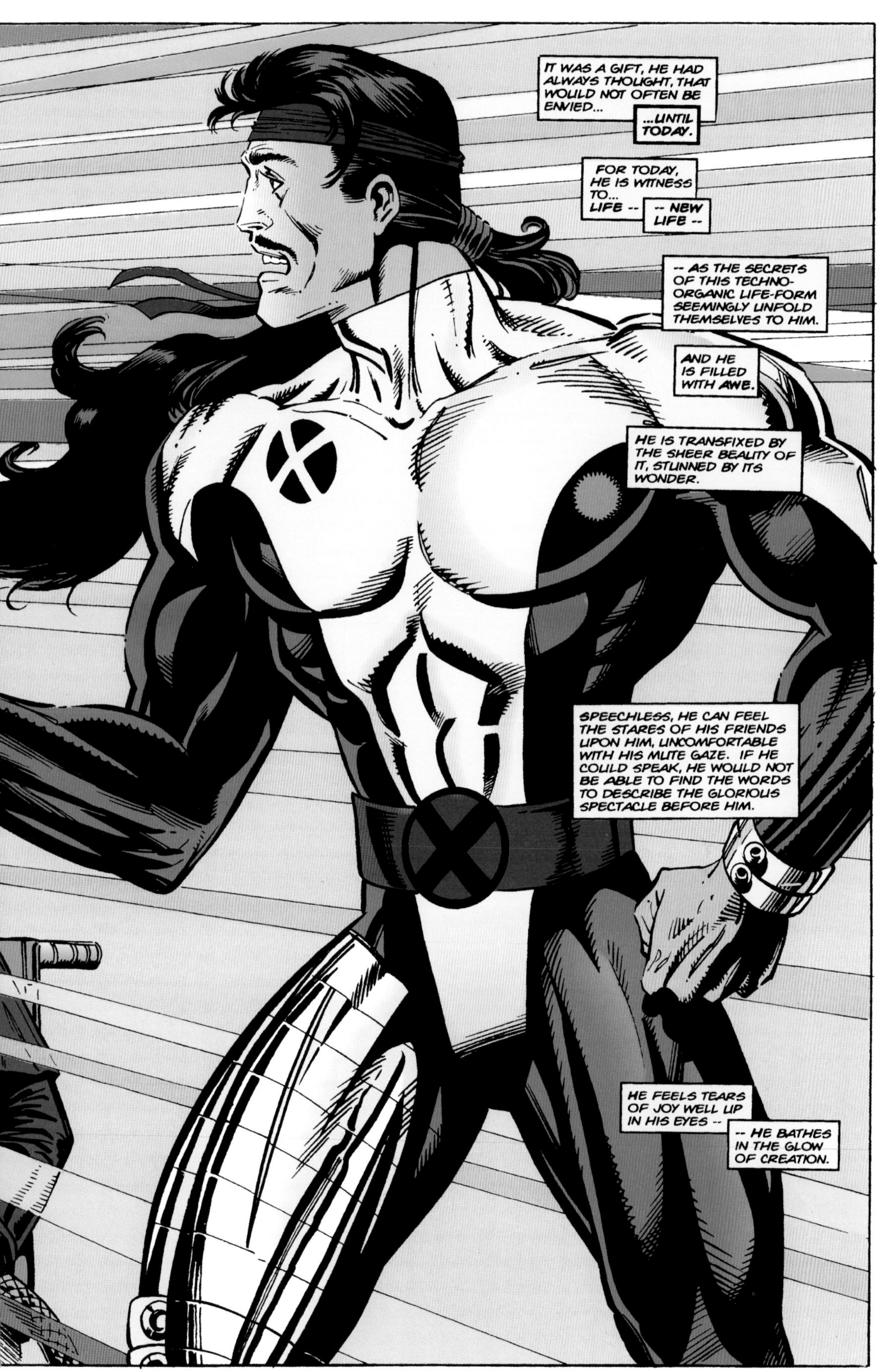
IT WAS A GIFT, HE HAD ALWAYS THOUGHT, THAT WOULD NOT OFTEN BE ENVIED...
...UNTIL TODAY.
FOR TODAY, HE IS WITNESS TO... LIFE --
-- NEW LIFE --
-- AS THE SECRETS OF THIS TECHNO-ORGANIC LIFE-FORM SEEMINGLY UNFOLD THEMSELVES TO HIM.
AND HE IS FILLED WITH AWE.
HE IS TRANSFIXED BY THE SHEER BEAUTY OF IT, STUNNED BY ITS WONDER.
SPEECHLESS, HE CAN FEEL THE STARES OF HIS FRIENDS UPON HIM, UNCOMFORTABLE WITH HIS MUTE GAZE. IF HE COULD SPEAK, HE WOULD NOT BE ABLE TO FIND THE WORDS TO DESCRIBE THE GLORIOUS SPECTACLE BEFORE HIM.
HE FEELS TEARS OF JOY WELL UP IN HIS EYES --
-- HE BATHES IN THE GLOW OF CREATION.

IT IS, HOWEVER, TOO SHORT A MOMENT.

TOO BRIEF A JOY.

FORGE? IS THERE SOME-THING --

THUD

UNGH

ARE YOU ALL RIGHT? DID THAT "DOUG-THING" --?

NO, I'LL BE *FINE*.

WHEN I LOOKED AT THE PHALANX -- *DOUGLOCK* -- MY POWER... TOOK OVER, AND BEGAN TO *ANALYZE*... *EVERYTHING* ABOUT HIM.

EVERY MICRO-CIRCUIT IN HIM BECAME CLEAR.

I ESTABLISHED CONTACT.

BUT EVEN WITHOUT *MEANING* TO, CHARLES'S TELEPATHIC MIND IS CONSTANTLY WORKING ON *SOME* LEVEL -- ALBEIT LOW.

WHEN THE PROFESSOR'S AND MY POWERS *CROSSED*, IT CREATED A *RIFT*...

...AND I CAUGHT THE *FEED-BACK*.

CHARLES, WOULD IT BE TOO MUCH TO *ASK* FOR YOU TO *LEAVE* THE ROOM...?

CERTAINLY NOT, MAKER.
SAM, RAHNE...? IF YOU WOULD BE SO KIND AS TO STAY HERE AND KEEP AN EYE ON THINGS...?
OF COURSE, PROFESSOR.
ALTHOUGH I DINNA SEE WHAT IT IS YE'RE WORRIED ABOOT. I'M SURE EVERYTHING IS GOIN' T'BE FINE ONCE FORGE FINDS DOUGLOCK TRULY IS DOUG.
NO PROBLEM, SIR.
VERY WELL THEN. IF YOU NEED ME, I'LL BE IN THE SANCTUARY.
ALL RIGHT, FIRST THING'S FIRST. I BELIEVE --
AH BELIEVE AH WANT SOME ANSWERS!
AN' IF THESE PHALANX THINGS ARE ONE BIG INTELLIGENCE, THEN AH BELIEVE THAT "DOUG" HERE CAN ANSWER 'EM!
AH WANNA KNOW WHAT THE PHALANX IS, WHAT THEY'VE DONE WITH THE X-MEN, AN' WHAT THEY'RE PLANNIN' T'DO!
AN' I WANNA KNOW RIGHT NOW...

'CAUSE AH GOT NO PATIENCE F'R ANY OF THIS --
-- AN' I GOT NO PATIENCE F'R YOU!
AH RESENT YOU F'R TAKIN' MY FRIEND'S FACE! AH RESENT YOU F'R PRETENDIN' HE COULD BE ALIVE AGAIN!
IF IT WILL ASSIST IN YOUR UNDERSTANDING AND ACCEPTANCE OF THE SITUATION, I WILL RELATE TO YOU THE INFORMATION YOU REQUIRE.
THE TECHNO-ORGANIC CREATURE SPREADS HIS ARMS AS IF TO EMBRACE THE WORLD, HIS ARMS AND FINGERS EXTENDING UNTIL THEY TOUCH OPPOSITE WALLS.
AND SUDDENLY, THE DANK STONE WALLS DISAPPEAR, REPLACED BY AN ENVELOPING COCOON OF TECHNO-ORGANIC CIRCUITRY.
SAM GUTHRIE DOES NOT LIKE BEING IN A ROOM WITH DOUGLOCK. HIS ANXIETY IS MAGNIFIED AS...
INDEED, DOUGLOCK HAS BECOME THE ROOM.
AH DON'T LIKE THIS...
DO NOT BE ALARMED.
THIS IS MERELY THE MOST EFFICIENT WAY I KNOW TO REVEAL THE HISTORY OF THE PHALANX ON THIS PLANET.
IT BEGAN SHORTLY AFTER THE DEATH OF THE TERRAN KNOWN AS DOUGLAS RAMSEY.

EMPLOYING MY HOLOGRAPHIC FIBER-OPTIC PROGRAM --
--YOU WILL HAVE FULL ACCESS TO ALL THE INFORMATION I POSSESS REGARDING THE EVOLUTION OF THE PHALANX.
SOON AFTER THE EVENTS OF THE SO-CALLED EXTINCTION AGENDA, THE GENOSHAN GOVERNMENT --
-- DESPERATE FOR FUNDS AFTER LOSING THEIR ECONOMIC BASE FOLLOWING THE LIBERATION OF THEIR MUTATE POPULATION --
-- SOLD THE GENETIC REMAINS OF THIS UNIT.
<CORRECTION:> -- THE GENETIC REMAINS OF THE TECHNO-ORGANIC EXTRATERRESTRIAL DESIGNATE: WARLOCK, TO AN UNKNOWN THIRD PARTY, CONSISTING OF MEMBERS IN THE HIGHEST CIRCLES OF THE TERRAN SCIENTIFIC COMMUNITY.
THESE HUMAN SCIENTISTS WERE DETERMINED TO USE THE TECHNO-ORGANIC MATERIAL FOR THEIR OWN MEANS...
...THE CREATION OF A NEW BREED OF SENTIENT "LIVING SENTINELS."
UPON BEING ABLE TO DUPLICATE THE TRANSMODE VIRUS CAPABLE OF TRANSFORMING LIVING MATTER INTO TECHNO-ORGANICS...
...THEY BELIEVED THEY HELD THE KEY TO SAVING THE ENTIRE "HUMAN" RACE FROM MUTANT SUPPLANTATION.
IN ACTUALITY, THEY MORE LIKELY THAN NOT DOOMED EVERY LIVING ENTITY ON THE PLANET.
THEIR FIRST MISTAKE MAY HAVE COME IN THE ENLISTMENT OF THE DR. STEVEN LANG.
ONCE A BRILLIANT SCIENTIST IN CHARGE OF THE PROJECT ARMAGEDDON (A PRECURSOR TO THE GOVERNMENT'S CURRENT "MUTANT CONTAINMENT PROGRAM," PROJECT: WIDEAWAKE)...
...HE WAS TRACKED TO A CONVALESCENT HOME, A MAN BROKEN IN BODY AS WELL AS SPIRIT.

BECAUSE OF HIS BRIEF ASSOCIATION WITH THE CYBERNETIC BRAIN NET OF THE SENTINEL CALLED MASTER MOLD --
-- IT WAS DETERMINED DESIGNATE: LANG WAS THE BEST CANDIDATE TO SERVE AS A CARBON-BASED REPOSITORY --
-- FOR THE COLLECTIVE INTELLIGENCE DESIGNED TO CONTROL THE HUNDREDS OF POTENTIAL SOLDIERS NEEDED AS THE FINAL SOLUTION FOR THE PROBLEM OF MUTANTS.
HIS MENTAL CONDITION DID NOT SEEM TO BOTHER THOSE RESPONSIBLE FOR HIS ABDUCTION...
...FOR SURELY THE PROCESS THAT FOLLOWED WOULD HAVE DRIVEN HIM INSANE IN ANY CASE ONCE IT WAS COMPLETED.
YOU'RE SAYING ALL THE THOUGHTS AND ACTIONS OF THE PHALANX ARE BEING CHANNELED THROUGH ONE MIND?
ACCH, THE POOR MAN -- EVEN THE DEVIL HIMSELF SHOULDNAE HAVE T'SUFFER SO!
WHAT'S THE DEAL WITH THIS HOLOGRAPHIC IMAGE...?
DID ROGUE EVER BATTLE THE PHALANX?
IN A FASHION, YES. SHE BATTLED THE EARLIEST PROTOTYPES...
...ONES CREATED WHOLE CLOTH FROM LANG'S TORTURED MIND.

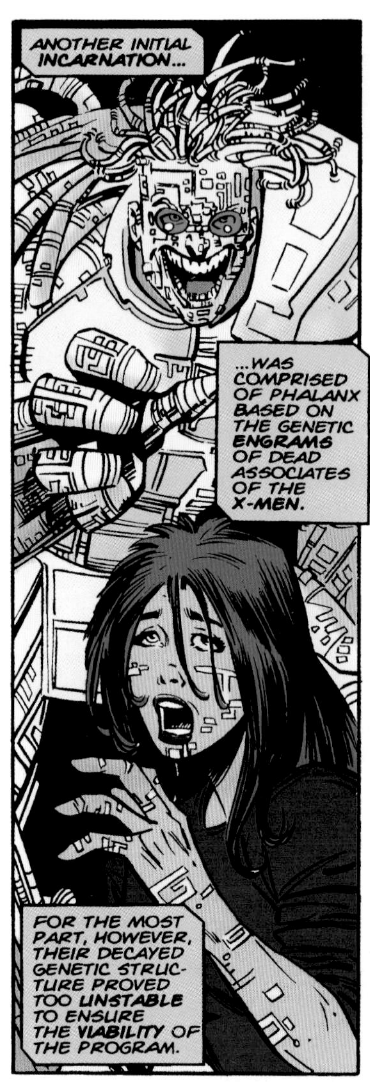
ANOTHER INITIAL INCARNATION...
...WAS COMPRISED OF PHALANX BASED ON THE GENETIC ENGRAMS OF DEAD ASSOCIATES OF THE X-MEN.
FOR THE MOST PART, HOWEVER, THEIR DECAYED GENETIC STRUCTURE PROVED TOO UNSTABLE TO ENSURE THE VIABILITY OF THE PROGRAM.

IT WAS THEN DECIDED HUMAN VOLUNTEERS WERE NEEDED. RECRUITS WERE FOUND AMONG THE RADICAL FRINGE OF SUCH GROUPS AS THE FRIENDS OF HUMANITY.
MEN AND WOMEN DETERMINED TO DO ANYTHING TO PROTECT HUMANITY FROM MUTANT KIND...
PHALANX

...EVEN IF IT MEANT SACRIFICING THAT HUMANITY ALL TOGETHER!
THE PLAN TO SIMPLY ASSIMILATE ALL MUTANTS INTO THE COLLECTIVE INTELLIGENCE PROVED IMPOSSIBLE --
-- WHEN IT WAS DETERMINED THAT HOMO SUPERIORS RESISTED THE TRANS-MODE VIRUS ON A DIONUCLEAIC LEVEL.

IF THAT'S TRUE -- AND I'M NOT CONVINCED ANYTHING YA'VE SAID IS TRUE --
-- WHY'VE THEY... WHY HAVE YOU... KIDNAPPED THE X-MEN AND TARGETED A HANDFUL O' INNOCENT NEW MUTANTS?

THEY PLAN TO EXPERIMENT ON THEM IN ORDER TO LEARN HOW TO ABSORB MUTANTS INTO THE PHALANX.
...THAT MUCH SEEMS CLEAR.
THE MYSTERY I WANT RESOLVED ...IS WHAT ABOUT YOU, "DOUGLOCK"?
HOW DID YOU MANAGE TO BREAK FREE OF THE COLLECTIVE INTELLIGENCE?

I AM RELATIVELY CERTAIN THE ANSWER TO THAT IS TWO-FOLD, FORGE.
FROM THE BEGINNING, I WAS ABLE TO MOUNT AT LEAST MARGINAL RESISTANCE AGAINST LANG...
...OWING, IN PART, TO THE FACT THAT -- AS THE MEMBER OF THE PHALANX BASED ON THE ENGRAMS OF THE TRANS-MODE INFECTED DOUGLAS RAMSEY --
-- AND ONE OF THE EARLIEST PHALANX DERIVED FROM THE GENOSHAN SAMPLE --
-- I POSSESS A CONSCIENCE-TEMPLATE CLOSEST TO MY ORIGINAL INCARNATION.
THOUGH I AM CERTAIN I WOULD NOT HAVE BEEN FREED AT ALL, IF I WERE NOT CONTACTED THROUGH THE CYBER-NET --
-- BY THE STRYFE-CREATED SENTIENT UNIT-DESIGNATE: ZERO.
CLAIMING HE SENSED "SOMETHING" IN ME THAT EVEN I DID NOT KNOW EXISTED, HE LIBERATED ME FROM THE COLLECTIVE INTELLIGENCE.*
IT WAS ONLY AFTER I WAS FREE OF THE PHALANX, THAT I LEARNED THE TRUTH...
* SEE EXCALIBUR # 80 - 82 -- Kel.
...THAT EVERY MEMBER OF THE GROUP IS FOLLOWING A GENETIC IMPERATIVE MUCH STRONGER THAN THAT PROGRAMMED BY THE HUMANS.
THEY ARE FOLLOWING SOMETHING NO HUMAN CAN COMPREHEND -- THE CALL OF A SPECIES NOT OF THIS WORLD.
THE PHALANX IS GROWING.
ADAPTING.
CHANGING.
IT IS RESPONDING TO "TRAITS" LEFT OVER BY THE FATHER RACE THAT BIRTHED IT AMONG THE STARS.
A RACE FOUNDED ON THE TOTAL AND COMPLETE GENOCIDE OF ALL LIVING MATTER THROUGHOUT THE UNIVERSE.
SO YA SAYING THAT NO MATTER WHAT THEY STARTED OUT AS, THESE "LIVING SENTINELS"...
...HAVE BECOME THE HARBINGERS OF THE END OF THE WORLD. MAKES SENSE.
WARLOCK'S PEOPLE WERE, BY NATURE, BARBARIC CONQUERORS.
IF THE PHALANX ARE BASED ON THEIR TEMPLATE, PURE ORGANIC LIFE WOULD BE ANATHEMA TO THEM.
THE PHALANX ARE UNDER NO ONE'S CONTROL -- BUT THEIR OWN?

AS AM I.
AND I HAVE NEED OF YOU, MAKER --
SHOOP
UNH.
-- FOR YOU PLAY A VERY PROMINENT PART IN MY PLANS.
WITH YOUR "SIGHT," I WILL BE ABLE TO GLEAN NEW INFORMATION ABOUT THE PHALANX THAT EVEN THEY ARE UNAWARE OF.
WHUD

AH KNEW WE SHOULDN'T 'AVE TRUSTED YOU.
IT DIDN'T TAKE LONG F'R YA T'FINALLY SHOW YER TRUE COL -- huh?
SHOOM
SPLARCH
THOOMP
YOUR SUSPICIOUS NATURE AND LACK OF TRUST CAUSE YOU TO ACT RASHLY, SAM GUTHRIE.
NOW THAT I HAVE ACQUIRED THE MAKER, IT IS IMPERATIVE THAT WE LEAVE IMMEDIATELY WITH --

NO! DOUG, STOP THIS!

I DINNA KEN WHY YE'RE DOIN' THIS, BUT TAKE ME WITH YE, DOUG --
-- WHEREVER YE'RE GOIN'... I BELIEVE IN YE! I BELIEVE THAT, NO MATTER WHAT IT LOOKS LIKE YE'RE DOIN' --
THAT YE'D EVER DO ANYTHING T'HURT ANY O'YUIR FRIENDS...
HE CAN HEAR IT IN THE TIMBRE OF HER VOICE, AN UNQUESTIONING CERTAINTY...
...THAT THESE ARE PEOPLE THAT HE SHOULD CONSIDER HIS FRIENDS...
...PEOPLE HE SHOULD CARE FOR...
...IF HE WERE CAPABLE OF CARING.
VERY WELL.

AND ABOVE...
I'M GONNA TELL THE PROFESSOR ...NEXT TIME HE GETS IN MY HEAD AN' YELLS -- "SAM'S IN TROUBLE! GET DOWNSTAIRS!" -- HE'S GONNA HAFTA TURN DOWN THE VOLUME!
MY NOGGIN IS STILL RINGIN' WI --
WAKT
BAMF
CHOOM
OOF!
AMBUSHED.
BY THE PHALANX... BUT IS IT --
BAMF
DOUG-LOCK...?
IS THAT YOU?
WHAT HAVE YOU DONE WITH --
MEIN GOTT!

I HAVE NEITHER THE TIME NOR THE DESIRE TO EXPLAIN MY ACTIONS TO YOU. SUFFICE IT TO SAY, I WILL BE LEAVING THIS FACILITY IMMEDIATELY.
ANY ATTEMPTS TO STOP ME WOULD BE FUTILE.
WHAT HAVE YOU DONE !?!
AFTER DOUGLOCK'S APPEARANCE MERE DAYS AGO, NIGHTCRAWLER HAD REGARDED HIM AS YET ANOTHER OF THE MANY CURIOSITIES HE HAS SEEN IN HIS LIFE.
HE, ALONG WITH THE REST OF EXCALIBUR, HAD JUST BEGUN TO ACCEPT DOUGLOCK, A DECISION THAT REQUIRED A CONSIDERABLE AMOUNT OF TRUST.
NOW, THAT TRUST IS BETRAYED, AND KURT WAGNER FEELS THE ANGER WELL UP INSIDE HIM.
BY FORCE OF WILL, HE TRIGGERS HIS MUTANT ABILITY TO TELEPORT --
FUMPH FUMPH FUMPH FUMPH
CRK CRKL CLK CK
AARGH!
-- ONLY TO BE DENIED, HIS POWER SEEMINGLY "FLIPPING" BACK INTO ITSELF, A WAVE OF INCREDIBLE PAIN WASHING OVER HIM.
CAN BARELY MOVE.
DOUGLOCK MUST HAVE SOMEHOW MANIPULATED THE PERIPHERAL ELECTROMAGNETIC FIELD, CONTAINING MY POWER, MAKING IT IMPOSSIBLE FOR ME TO TELEPORT ANYWHERE.
HE ANALYZED MY POWER AND THEN USED IT AGAINST ME. HE MUST HAVE BEEN WORKING FOR THE PHALANX ALL ALONG.
WHY THEN DOES HE LOOK SO... SAD...AND ANXIOUS?

EEEEEEAAAAAAH!
111100010 110 00 100
THERE IS PAIN -- OR AT LEAST THE MEMORY OF PAIN -- AS DOUGLOCK'S OWN ELECTRO-MAGNETIC AURA TIGHTENS AROUND HIM --
--CONSTRICTING HIM --
-- PARALYZING HIM --
THAT'S AS FAR AS YOU GO, DOUG-LOCK!
YOU HURT KURT, BY DISRUPTING HIS E.M. FIELD -- I KNOW, I FELT YOU DO IT --
DON'T MAKE ME DO THE SAME TO YOU.
SHE COULD EASILY TEAR HIM APART WITH THE AWESOME ENERGY SHE WIELDS. IN FACT, IT TAKES MORE EFFORT ON POLARIS'S PART TO HOLD BACK THE MAGNETIC POWER THAN EXERT IT.
SHE TIGHTENS HER HOLD A LITTLE TO ASSURE HIS CAPTIVITY.
-:UNGH:- -- IN YOUR -- EFFORT TO CONTAIN -- ME, YOU HAVE FAILED TO NOTICE YOUR TEAMMATES HAVE BEEN -- BONDED TO ME.
THE FORCE -- YOU INFLICT ON ME, IS FELT BY THEM AS WELL.
SHE HESITATES...
SWAKK
...CREATING AN OPENING DOUG-LOCK SWIFTLY USES TO HIS ADVANTAGE.

WHOA!
GO LIMP, POLARIS, I'VE GOT YOU!
-UNGH!-
WAIT, RICTOR!
I CAN SENSE AN ANOMALY IN THE --
BY THE GODS!
HOLY --
THEY ARE AS STUNNED BY THE DEAFENING EXPLOSION...

...AS THEY ARE BY THE HORRIFIC SIGHT THAT GREETS THEM.
DON'T APPROACH ME. I DO WHAT I MUST.
BABEL AWAITS...AND BABEL MUST BE STOPPED.
KITTY! DO NOT CONFRONT DOUGLOCK!
UNTIL WE CAN DISCOVER HIS INTENTIONS, WE MUST CONSIDER HIM DANGEROUS!
BUT PROFESSOR, HE'S GOT SAM, RAHNE, AND FORGE! WE CAN'T JUST LET HIM --
AT THIS POINT I CAN ASCERTAIN THAT, THOUGH UNCONSCIOUS, THEY REMAIN UNINJURED. HOWEVER, MY ORDER STANDS...
DO NOT APPROACH HIM!!!
IN THE DAYS SINCE HIS INTRODUCTION TO THE TEAM EXCALIBUR, DOUGLOCK HAS REPEATEDLY PROCLAIMED HIS INHUMANITY --
-- CATEGORICALLY REFUTING ANY SIMILARITY HIS TEAMMATES MAY HAVE SEEN BETWEEN HIMSELF AND THE DECEASED DOUG RAMSEY.
HE IS AN ENGRAM ONLY, PHALANX-BORN, BASED ON THE GENETIC AND MENTAL IMPRINTS OF RAMSEY.
HE FOUND THAT DUE TO THIS RESEMBLANCE, THEY LENT HIM A CERTAIN ACCEPTANCE, A MEASURE OF TRUST...
BUT IF INDEED HE IS OF PHALANX, LACKING IN HUMAN EMOTION...

...WHY THEN DOES HE FEEL THE "SORROW"...
DOUGLOCK, WAIT!
...OF SHAKING THEIR FAITH IN HIM?

SHHHHHUNK!

WHERE DID HE GO, PROFESSOR?
WHERE DID THEY GO?
I CANNOT LOCATE ANY OF THEM.
THEY'RE GONE...
...AND I FEAR THAT THEY MAY HAVE TAKEN OUR ONLY HOPE OF DEFEATING THE PHALANX WITH THEM...
CONTINUED IN X-FORCE #38
Phalanx Covenant
LIFESIGNS PART 2

APPROVED BY THE COMICS CODE AUTHORITY
TONY DANIEL 94
KEVIN CONRAD

MARVEL COMICS
$2.95 US
$4.00 CAN
38
SEP
X-FORCE
X-MEN EVENT
PHALANX COVENANT
LIFE SIGNS
PART 2

BONUS LIFESIGNS PIN-UP
X-TEAMS UNITE...
...the Phalanx Covenant HAS BEGUN!

THE PHALANX COVENANT
FEATURING X-FACTOR, X-FORCE AND EXCALIBUR
SO, "DOUGLOCK"--
--THIS IS THE "SUPER-SECRET HEADQUARTERS" OF THE GROUP THAT'S POSIN'A THREAT TA LIFE ON EARTH AS WE KNOW IT, HUH?

FABIAN NICIEZA WRITER | TONY DANIEL PENCILER | KEVIN CONRAD INKER | CHRIS ELIOPOULOS LETTERER | MARIE JAVINS COLORIST | BOB HARRAS EDITOR | TOM DeFALCO EDITOR IN CHIEF

BOOK TWO

FORGE, CANNONBALL AND WOLFSBANE WERE BROUGHT TO THIS BEAUTIFUL HAMLET IN THE HEART OF THE ITALIAN ALPS--
--BY A TECHNO-ORGANIC BEING WHO HAS ASSUMED THE FORM, IF NOT THE ESSENCE--
--OF THEIR DECEASED FRIEND AND FORMER NEW MUTANT TEAMMATE, DOUG RAMSEY.
SCOTTY'S
FARMER'S FOODS
PORK&BACON

STAN LEE PRESENTS

PART TWO

Cannonball

Boomer

Siryn

Warpath

Rictor

Shatterstar

Forge

Polaris

LIFE SIGNS

DOUGLOCK, AS HE HAS COME TO BE NAMED, IS A RENEGADE MEMBER OF A NEW AND DEADLY LIFEFORM, KNOW AS THE PHALANX --

-- WHICH SEEKS TO SPREAD ACROSS THE WORLD, ASSIMILATING ALL SPECIES OF LIVING CREATURES INTO THEIR ARTIFICIAL COLLECTIVE INTELLIGENCE.

DOUGLOCK SOMEHOW BROKE FREE FROM THAT GROUP-MIND, SOUGHT INDEPENDENCE, AND USING THE TRACE MEMORIES OF THE BEING HE HAD ONCE BEEN --

-- SOUGHT TO WARN OTHERS OF THE PHALANX THREAT.*

*A VERY CONDENSED VERSION OF EVENTS IN EXCALIBUR 77-80. --BOB

Nightcrawler

Shadowcat

Meggan

Daytripper

Britanic

THE FAITH DANCERS

Havok

Strong Guy

Wolfsbane

HIS RETURN HAS STIRRED UP A VARIETY OF EMOTIONS IN THOSE THE REAL DOUG RAMSEY ONCE KNEW AND LOVED...
...AND WHO, ONCE, LOVED HIM BACK.
SAMUEL GUTHRIE [SUB-DESIGNATE CANNONBALL]--INTERROGATIVE QUERY: WHAT HAS THIS ENTITY DONE TO FOSTER SUCH DISTRUST IN YOU--
--AND YET ENGENDER SUCH FRIENDSHIP IN RAHNE SINCLAIR [SUB-DESIGNATE WOLFSBANE]--?
LET'S JUS' SAY THAT YOU'VE GIVEN US MORE N' ENOUGH REASON TA DOUBT THAN TA WELCOME YOU BACK WITH OPEN ARMS.
YOU SHOW UP A FEW DAYS AGO SAYIN' YOU'RE SOMEONE AH SAW DIE WITH MAH OWN TWO EYES--
--SOMEONE WHO WAS MY FRIEND. DO Y'UNDERSTAND--MY FRIEND!?
AH THINK AH HAVE THE RIGHT T'BE A LITTLE SKEPTICAL.
AN' THE X-MEN ARE MISSIN', KIDNAPPED BY YOUR TECHNO-MATES, THE PHALANX--
--NEXT THEY TOOK OVER MUIR ISLAND AS WELL.
FORCIN' EXCALIBUR TO CALL THE REST O' US TOGETHER AT THE MONASTERY AT MONT ST. FRANCIS, TURNIN' IT INTO OUR OWN VERSION A' THE ALAMO.
AN' THEN YOU DECIDE IT'S AS GOOD A TIME AS ANY TO WRAP YOURSELF ALL OVER FORGE LIKE WET FUR ON A HOUND DOG, BONDIN' WITH HIM IN YOUR OWN SPECIAL PHALANX WAY--
--LEAVIN' HIM TWO OARS SHY A' ROWIN' THE BOAT.
YOU LEAD US CLEAR ACROSS EUROPE TO HERE--
--TELLIN' US THIS PLACE REPRESENTS A DANGER TO ALL HUMAN LIFE.
YOU TOLD US, "DOUG," THAT EVERYTHIN' DEPENDED ON US COMIN' HERE. AN' WHEN WE DIDN'T BELIEVE YOU, YOU TOOK US!

AH JUST THINK IT'S TIME YOU PROVED YOUR POINT, BOY.
YOUR INTERPRETATION OF RECENT EVENTS IS ACCURATE FROM A CHRONOLOGICAL STANDPOINT--
--THOUGH YOUR PERCEPTION OF THE MOTIVATIONAL INFLUENCES WHICH HAVE DRIVEN US TO THIS POINT--
--ARE SUBJECT TO DISAGREEMENT ON MY PART.
THEN PROVE ONE THING T'ME, PHALANX--PROVE ONE THING YOU SAID WAS TRUE!
SAMUEL GUTHRIE!
HOW COULD YE BE SO MISTRUSTFUL?
THE VERY FACT THAT DOUG IS STANDIN' IN FRONT O' US--
--IS SIGN ENOUGH THAT WE SHOULD BE HELPING HIM!
HAVE YE BECOME SO BLIND AND CYNICAL WORKIN' WITH THE LIKES O' CABLE--
--CAN YOU NAE APPRECIATE A MIRACLE WHEN YE SEE ONE?!

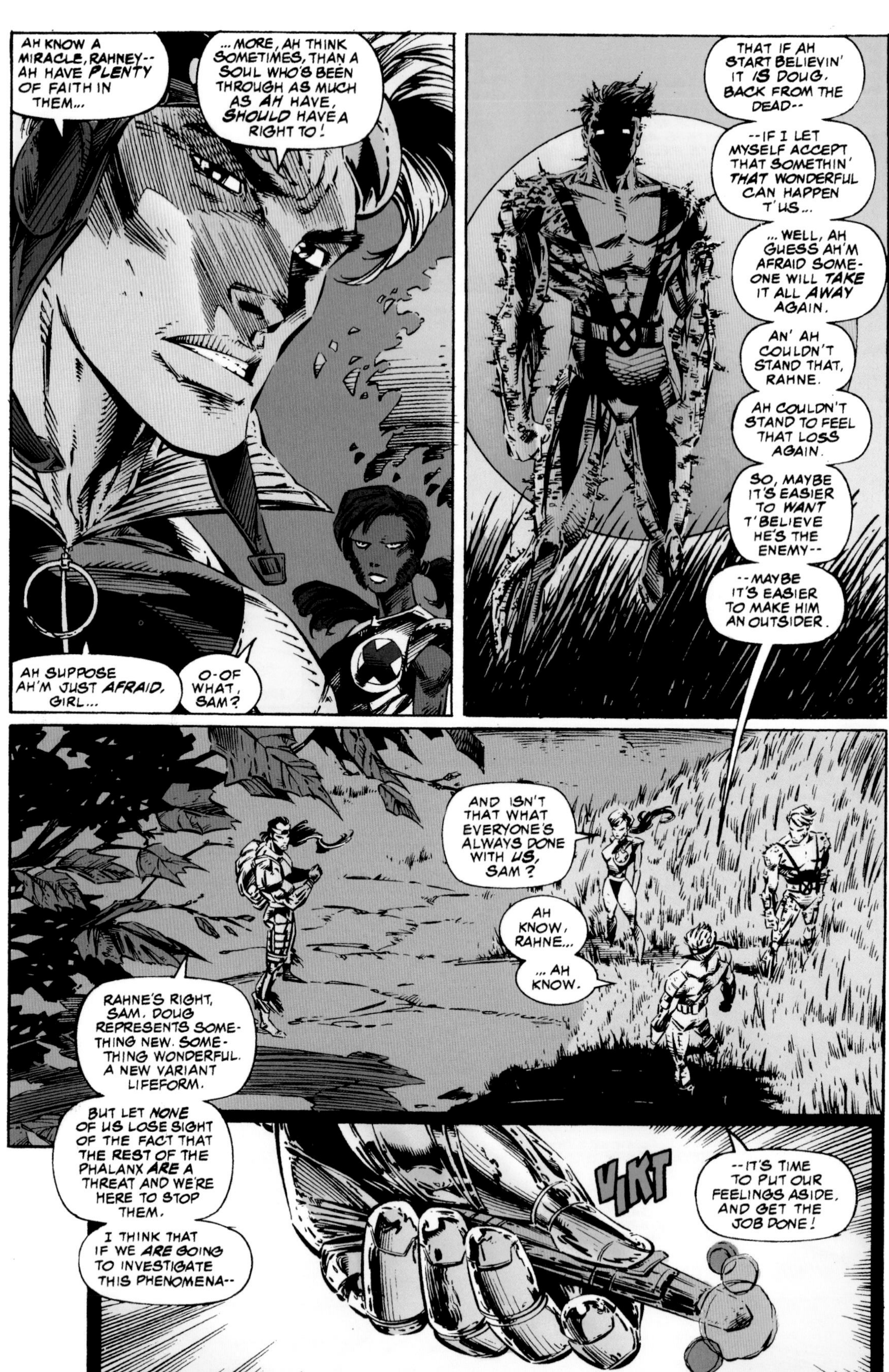
AH KNOW A MIRACLE, RAHNEY-- AH HAVE PLENTY OF FAITH IN THEM...
...MORE, AH THINK SOMETIMES, THAN A SOUL WHO'S BEEN THROUGH AS MUCH AS AH HAVE, SHOULD HAVE A RIGHT TO!
AH SUPPOSE AH'M JUST AFRAID, GIRL...
O-OF WHAT, SAM?
THAT IF AH START BELIEVIN' IT IS DOUG, BACK FROM THE DEAD--
--IF I LET MYSELF ACCEPT THAT SOMETHIN' THAT WONDERFUL CAN HAPPEN T'US...
...WELL, AH GUESS AH'M AFRAID SOME-ONE WILL TAKE IT ALL AWAY AGAIN.
AN' AH COULDN'T STAND THAT, RAHNE.
AH COULDN'T STAND TO FEEL THAT LOSS AGAIN.
SO, MAYBE IT'S EASIER TO WANT T'BELIEVE HE'S THE ENEMY--
--MAYBE IT'S EASIER TO MAKE HIM AN OUTSIDER.
AND ISN'T THAT WHAT EVERYONE'S ALWAYS DONE WITH US, SAM?
AH KNOW, RAHNE...
...AH KNOW.
RAHNE'S RIGHT, SAM. DOUG REPRESENTS SOME-THING NEW. SOME-THING WONDERFUL. A NEW VARIANT LIFEFORM.
BUT LET NONE OF US LOSE SIGHT OF THE FACT THAT THE REST OF THE PHALANX ARE A THREAT AND WE'RE HERE TO STOP THEM.
I THINK THAT IF WE ARE GOING TO INVESTIGATE THIS PHENOMENA--
VIKT
--IT'S TIME TO PUT OUR FEELINGS ASIDE. AND GET THE JOB DONE!

WAIT A MINUTE, AH DON'T MEAN T'BE RUDE, BUT JUST LIKE THAT ?
SHOULDN'T WE HAVE A PLAN ?
DOUGLOCK BROUGHT US HERE FOR A REASON, SAM.
THE PHALANX HAVE TO BE STOPPED...
...AND IF THIS TOWN IS WHERE WE NEED TO GO TO DO THAT...
... THEN THE MOST LOGICAL THING TO DO IS TO SIMPLY PUT ONE FOOT IN FRONT OF THE OTHER, RIGHT?
SO HOW COME I FEEL LIKE I'M WALKIN' INTO THE LION'S DEN ?
DINNAE BE SILLY! DOUG WOULD NAE LET US BE HURT !
WHY, LOOK AT THIS PLACE, SAM! 'TIS AN ABSOLUTELY PERFECT VILLAGE!

YEAH... ALMOST TOO PERFECT.
HOW COME NO ONE'S EVEN GIVIN' US A SECOND GLANCE?
AH MEAN, WE DO KINDA STICK OUT!
MUSTARD
PUB
ACTUALLY, SAM, THAT WOULD BE MY DOING.
THE LITTLE GIZMO I WAS COBBLING TOGETHER WHILE ALL OF YOU WERE ARGUING--
--IS A HOLOGRAPHIC TRANSMITTER.
EVERYONE IN TOWN IS SEEING US JUST THE WAY I WANT THEM TO.
AN' WE'LL RUN INTO THE BODY SNATCHER PODS 'ROUND THE NEXT CORNER, AH'LL BET!
I DO NOT UNDERSTAND THE ANALOGY.
EVERYTHING AROUND HERE LOOKS TOO GOOD, DOUG--UHM... LOCK... TOO NORMAL.
IT'S LIKE THE ENTIRE PLACE IS SOME KIND OF FREAKY MOVIE SET...

IF ANYTHING, SAMUEL, THE PHALANX INFESTATION DOES NOT APPEAR TO BE VERY LARGE AT THIS LOCATION.
BUT APPEARANCES, I CONCUR, CAN BE DECEIVING.
YOU CAN SEE SOMETHING WHICH OUR EYES CAN'T, "DOUG"?
THEY ARE HERE. ALL AROUND US.
I CAN SENSE THE BUZZING DRONE OF THE COLLECTIVE INTELLIGENCE--
--RINGING IN THE BACK OF MY SELF-ACTUALIZATION NEUROSYNAPTIC NETWORK.

AND ALTHOUGH I WAS REMOVED FROM THE HIVE--

--AND SOUGHT REFUGE BEYOND THE COVENANT--
--THIS UNIT WOULD ANTICIPATE, THAT IF IT CAN SEE THEM...

...THEN MOST CERTAINLY IT WOULD STAND TO REASON...
...THEY, TOO, CAN SEE US!

NORMANDY. MONT ST. FRANCIS.
IN ITS TIME, IT HAS BEEN BOTH A HOME OF RELIGIOUS STUDY AND A PLACE OF REFUGE.
THIS MONASTERY HAS STOOD, IN ONE FORM OR ANOTHER, ON THIS SPOT FOR CLOSE TO A MILLENNIUM.
IT HAS EVER BEEN A PLACE OF LEGEND. FOLKLORE CALLS IT A MAGICKAL SITE.
PERHAPS. PERHAPS NOT.
FOR THIS DAY, THEY STAND AS THE LAST BASTION OF HOPE MANKIND HAS LEFT AGAINST THE PHALANX HORDE.
THE MOUNT, ONCE MORE, IS A PLACE OF REFUGE.
IF MAGIC WAS THERE, IT FAILED WHEN THE NAZIS OCCUPIED THIS PORTION OF FRANCE DURING WORLD WAR II. THE MONASTIC ORDER THAT HAD LIVED HERE FROM THE BEGINNING WAS FORCED TO FLEE.
THEY NEVER RETURNED.
THE MONASTERY REMAINED ABANDONED, UNTIL THE MEGALO-MANIACAL FABIAN CORTEZ--FORMER LEADER OF MAGNETO'S DEVOTED ACOLYTES--MOVED HIS FLOCK OF WORSHIPPERS HERE.
THE ACOLYTES ARE GONE, REPLACED BY ANOTHER GROUP OF MUTANTS WHO HAVE COME HERE IN DESPERATION AND FEAR.

DR. MOIRA MACTAGGERT STANDS ALONGSIDE THE COLLECTIVE MUTANT TEAMS OF EXCALIBUR, X-FORCE AND X-FACTOR, HER INSIDES CHURNING, AS THEY STRUGGLE TO FIND A KEY TO THE THREAT POSED BY THE PHALANX.
AMANDA, PLEASE, CONTINUE T' TRY TO SOOTHE KITTY WITH YOUR SORCEROUS SPELLS AS BEST YE CAN.
THE MACHINERY FORGE WAS ABLE T'COBBLE TOGETHER, USIN' THE EQUIPMENT LEFT BEHIND BY THE ACOLYTES--
--IS SEEKIN' OUT A BIOLOGICAL REMNANT OF THE TRANSMODE VIRUS--
--IN ANYONE WHO HAD PREVIOUS CONTACT WITH THE TECHNO-ORGANIC BEINGS WARLOCK AND THE MAGUS!
AND, AFTER HAVING RUN RICTOR THROUGH YOUR TORTURE CHAMBER, "DOCTOR"--
--YOU INSIST ON INFLICTING THE SAME PAIN ON SHADOWCAT?

D'YE HAVE ANY BETTER IDEAS, SON, CONSIDERING THAT OUR ONLY OTHER SOURCE OF THE TECHNO-ORGANIC MESH --
DOUGLAS RAMSEY
YE REALLY DINNAE TRUST SCIENTISTS, DO YE, SHATTERSTAR?
HAVIN' BEEN SUBJECTED TO A VARIATION OF THIS INFERNAL DEVICE M'SELF, I'M WELL AWARE OF THE RISKS KITTY'S TAKING.
AND AS MUCH AS IT PAINS ME T'DO THIS, AS A SCIENTIST, I CANNAE THINK OF A BETTER MEANS TO STOP THESE PHALANX BEASTIES --
-- THAN TO SEEK AN ANSWER AT THE SOURCE: THE VERY CELLULAR STRUCTURE OF WHICH THEY ARE MADE.
-- NAMELY DOUGLOCK, UP AN' DISAPPEARED?
I RATHER THOUGHT NOT.
SO, IF YOU PLEASE, DINNAE ACCUSE ME OF BEING INDIFFERENT TO THE PEOPLE I CARE ABOUT!
OF COURSE WE KNOW YOU'RE NOT, MOIRA.
BUT IT IS HARD T'SEE OUR FRIENDS SUFFER. WHY DOES IT ALWAYS SEEM NECESSARY FOR US TO SACRIFICE SO MUCH OF OURSELVES, BODY AND SOUL, TIME AND AGAIN?
I THOUGHT THAT WAS STANDARD OPERATING PROCEDURE AS FAR AS THE X-TEAMS WERE CONCERNED.
YOU REALLY SHOULD READ THE MANUAL THAT CAME WITH YOUR NEW COSTUME, DAYTRIPPER.
I WAS PRETTY SURE I KNEW WHAT I WAS GETTING INTO WHEN I JOINED EXCALIBUR, WARPATH...

"... BUT THE REALITY IS TOUGH TO HANDLE SOMETIMES."
LORNA... ANYTHING, YET?
IN ALL OF THE TWO MINUTES SINCE YOU ASKED LAST, ALEX?
NO. NOTHING.
THEY'VE BEEN IN THERE FOR HOURS NOW!
AN' KNOWIN' HOW STUBBORN THAT MAN CAN BE, HE'LL STAY THERE TILL HE FINDS WHAT HE'S LOOKING FOR!
AND THAT, SIRYN, IS BOTH WHAT ENDEARS US TO CHARLES XAVIER...
"...AND INTIMIDATES US SO MUCH, AS WELL!"
YOU'D THINK, AT LEAST, BY NOW, THAT HE'D BE CRAMPIN' UP BIG TIME!
THE PROFESSOR HAS NO FEELINGS IN HIS LEGS, GUIDO.
BUT HE MORE THAN MAKES UP FOR THAT LOSS WITH THOSE IN HIS HEART.
FOR THE SAKE OF BOTH HUMANS AND MUTANTS ALIKE --
-- THIS MAN WOULD SACRIFICE ALL HE HAS EVER WORKED FOR -- ALL HE HAS, IF NECESSARY --
-- IN ORDER TO SAVE THE WORLD!

GEEZ, NIGHTCRAWLER... I WAS JUST KIDDIN'.
THE PROFESSOR ASKED ME TA HELP CARRY 'IM UP THOSE BLASTED WINDING STONE STEPS--
--'CAUSE HIS HOVERCHAIR GOT TRASHED BY THE PHALANX.
HE SAID THAT MORE THAN ANY OF YOU OTHERS, I WOULD UNDERSTAND HIS FRUSTRATIONS OVER NEEDIN' "SUCH ASSISTANCE."
I TOLD HIM NOT T'WORRY. SAID I'D STAND WATCH OVER HIM TILL HE TELEPATHI-CALLY FOUND FORGE AND THE REST--
--OR UNTIL WE WERE ALL FOOD FOR THE WORMS! Y'KNOW WHAT I MEAN.
I DO.
MY APOLOGIES, GUIDO. I HAVE NO DOUBT YOU WILL DO JUST THAT!
JUST WATCH, KURT! LET ANY OF 'EM GIVE "KILLER CAROSELLA" A TRY!
I'LL MOIDERIZE 'EM!
JUGGERNAUT! HA! HE'S A LIGHTWEIGHT!
EXODUS! SHRUG HIM OFF LIKE WATER OFF A DUCK!
WHAT ABOUT THE IMPOSSIBLE MAN?
BAMF
THAT GREEN ALIEN PESTY GUY?
HIM, I'LL NEED HELP WITH.
HOLD YOUR NOSE AND HOLLER IF THERE'S ANY PROGRESS, MY FRIEND!
THE SULFUR STENCH FROM NIGHTCRAWLER'S TELEPORTATION WAFTS THROUGH THE AIR--
--BUT CHARLES XAVIER TAKES NO NOTICE.

FOR HE IS, IN TRUTH, FAR, FAR AWAY.
PHYSICALLY, HE REMAINS SEATED UNDER GUIDO'S CARE...
...BUT THE MIND OF THE GREATEST TELEPATH ON EARTH WANDERS FAR, FREE OF ALL PHYSICAL RE-STRAINTS--
--CHARLES XAVIER NOW CALMLY FLOATS THROUGH A DIFFERENT PART OF REALITY!
IT HAS BEEN A WHILE SINCE I VISITED THE SERENITY OF THE ASTRAL PLANE.
WOULD THAT I HAD TIME TO STROLL THROUGH IT IN TRAN-QUILITY.
BUT THAT IS A LUXURY THE X-MEN RARELY HAVE--
--AND EVEN LESS SO NOW, WITH THE PHALANX THREATENING TO OVERWHELM MAN AND MUTANT ALIKE ACROSS THE WORLD.
I NEED TO FIND FORGE AND "DOUG-LOCK," FOR I FEEL WITHIN THEM MAY BE THE ANSWERS WE NEED TO STOPPING THIS NEW THREAT.
LUCKILY, FINDING THE NEEDLE IN THE PROVERBIAL HAYSTACK OF MINDS I NOW SIFT THROUGH--
--IS MADE SLIGHTLY EASIER BY THE INTIMATE LEVEL OF KNOWLEDGE I POSSESS OF THOSE I SEARCH FOR!
THERE! SAM GUTHRIE! ANGRY... CONFUSED... PERHAPS A BIT FRIGHT-ENED...
...BUT THANKFULLY, HE APPEARS UNHURT.
AND WITH HIM IS FORGE, AS WELL.
HIS MIND IS ADRIFT, AS IF IN SOME SORT OF DREAM-STATE.
AND LAST, BUT NOT LEAST, RAHNE SINCLAIR.
SUCH HOPE AND WARMTH WITHIN HER, IT SHINES LIKE A BEACON.
THEY ARE ALL TOGETHER... AND THANKFULLY-- MERCIFULLY-- ALL STILL ALL RIGHT.

FORGE-- CAN YOU "HEAR" ME ?
CHAR... CHARLES? IS THAT YOU?
GOOD. I WAS WONDER...ING WHEN... YOU'D SHOW UP.
I NEED TO SEE WHERE YOU ARE, MY FRIEND... WHERE DOUGLOCK TOOK YOU.
TO UNDERSTAND EXACTLY WHY YOUR THOUGHTS ARE SO CHAOTIC, MAKER--
--I ASK THAT YOU ALLOW ME TO MERGE WITH YOUR CONSCIOUS MIND. I KNOW YOU ARE THE MOST PRIVATE OF MEN, AND I WOULD NOT ASK THIS IF THE SITUATION WERE NOT SO CRITICAL.
SURE... CHARLES... YOU JUST HAVE TO SEE...
...WHAT I'M... SEEING...
XAVIER'S MIND SLIPS INSIDE THAT OF THE MUTANT MAKER'S AND HIS EYES SNAP WIDE, AS IF HE HAD BEEN SLAPPED IN THE FACE.
THROUGH THE EYES OF FORGE, HE IS GIVEN A NEW OUTLOOK ON LIFE-- ONE HE HAS NEVER BEEN PRIVY TO.
INDEED, IN MANY WAYS CHARLES XAVIER HAS.
HE SEES, NOT ONLY THE PHALANX INFESTATION WITHIN THE SMALL ITALIAN HAMLET, BUT THE VERY SUBSTANCE OF REALITY ITSELF--
--THE WAY FORGE SEES.
AS AN INTERLOCKING, SYMBIOTIC EQUATION, WHERE LIVING TISSUE AND INORGANIC MATTER BECOME ONE.
WHERE EVERYTHING THAT EXISTS IS CREATED FROM THE SAME BASIC FOUNDATION--
--AND IT ALL RISES, ONE BUILDING BLOCK AFTER ANOTHER, IN AN ORDERLY, MATHEMATICAL PROGRESSION--
--TO BECOME WHAT IT WAS ALWAYS MEANT TO BECOME.

FORGE-- YOU OK.?
I NEVER REALIZED! THE WAY YOU SEE THINGS IS PURELY AMAZING.
YES. IT MAKES, CHARLES, FOR AN... INTERESTING... TIME...
... WHEN I TAKE A STROLL THROUGH A CROWDED APPLIANCE STORE!
DID Y'SAY "CHARLES"? IS PROFESSOR X IN CONTACT WITH YOU?
I AM, SAM. INSIDE FORGE'S MIND, SEEING THE WORLD AS HE DOES--
-- AND TRYING TO GAIN A NEW INSIGHT INTO THE CREATURES WE OPPOSE.
STARTING, I HOPE, WITH THE FACT THAT THEY AREN'T CREATURES!
THEY ARE SOMETHING... INCREDIBLE, CHARLES.
SOMETHING NEW!
AND MY FEAR, MAKER, IS THAT YOU ARE BEGINNING TO FEEL--
-- THAT THEY ARE ALSO SOMETHING BETTER!
DOUG, CAN YOU HELP THE PROFESSOR--
-- MAYBE SEE THE TRUTH ABOUT Y'SELF?
THAT WOULD BE A FRUITFUL ENDEAVOR, RAHNE SINCLAIR.
BY MERGING WITH ENTITY DESIGNATE: FORGE [SUB-DESIGNATE: THE MAKER]--
--THIS UNIT MAY BE CAPABLE OF PROVIDING A VALIDATION OF ITS OWN EXISTENCE--
--AND INDEED, THAT OF THE COLLECTIVE WHOLE, AS WELL.
WAIT A MINUTE! NOT IF IT MEANS INFECTING FORGE WITH THE TRANSMODE VIRUS, YOU AIN'T GONNA!

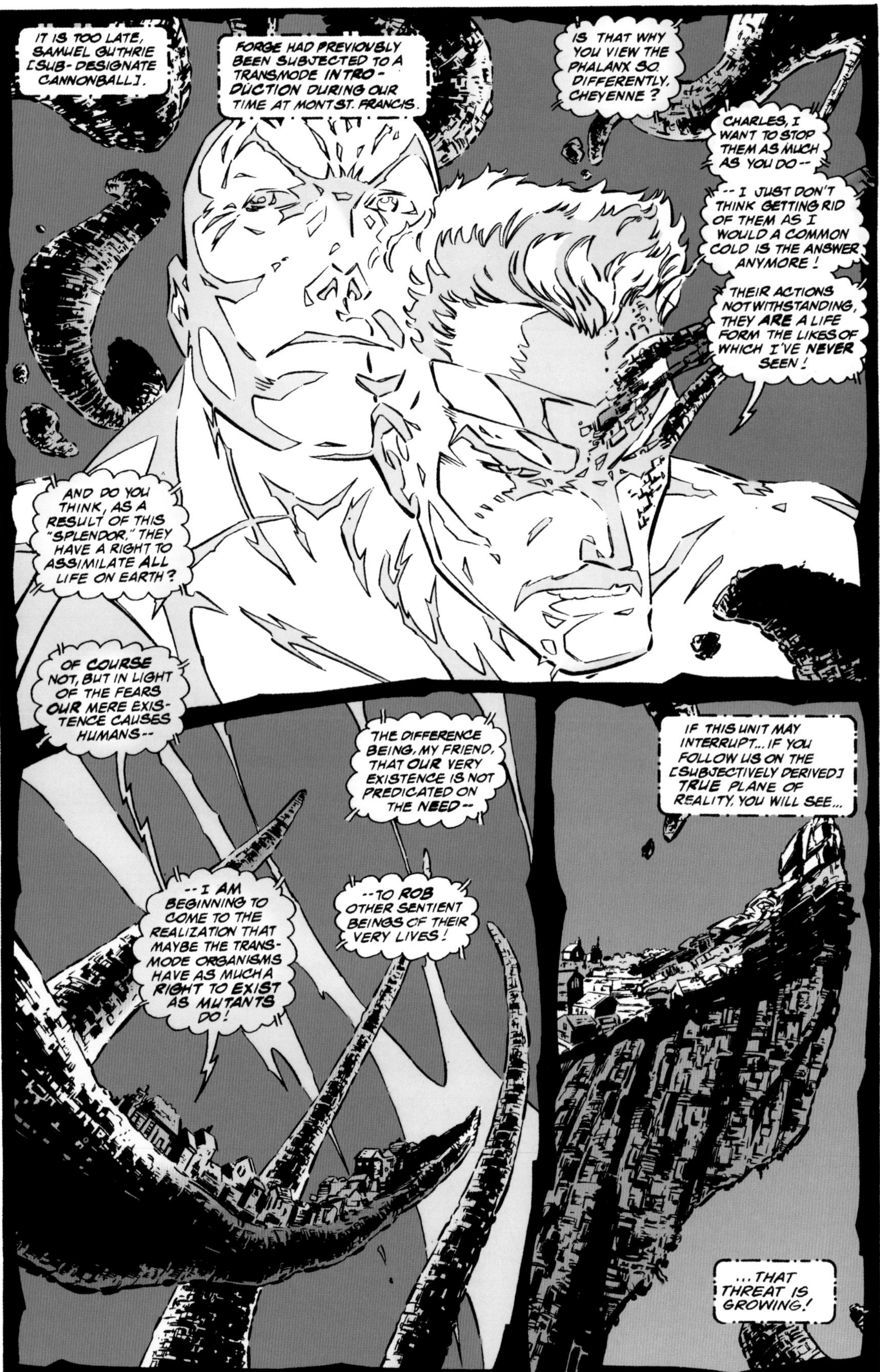
IT IS TOO LATE, SAMUEL GUTHRIE [SUB-DESIGNATE CANNONBALL].
FORGE HAD PREVIOUSLY BEEN SUBJECTED TO A TRANSMODE INTRO-DUCTION DURING OUR TIME AT MONT ST. FRANCIS.
IS THAT WHY YOU VIEW THE PHALANX SO DIFFERENTLY, CHEYENNE?
CHARLES, I WANT TO STOP THEM AS MUCH AS YOU DO--
--I JUST DON'T THINK GETTING RID OF THEM AS I WOULD A COMMON COLD IS THE ANSWER ANYMORE!
THEIR ACTIONS NOTWITHSTANDING, THEY ARE A LIFE FORM THE LIKES OF WHICH I'VE NEVER SEEN!
AND DO YOU THINK, AS A RESULT OF THIS "SPLENDOR," THEY HAVE A RIGHT TO ASSIMILATE ALL LIFE ON EARTH?
OF COURSE NOT, BUT IN LIGHT OF THE FEARS OUR MERE EXIS-TENCE CAUSES HUMANS--
--I AM BEGINNING TO COME TO THE REALIZATION THAT MAYBE THE TRANS-MODE ORGANISMS HAVE AS MUCH A RIGHT TO EXIST AS MUTANTS DO!
THE DIFFERENCE BEING, MY FRIEND, THAT OUR VERY EXISTENCE IS NOT PREDICATED ON THE NEED--
--TO ROB OTHER SENTIENT BEINGS OF THEIR VERY LIVES!
IF THIS UNIT MAY INTERRUPT... IF YOU FOLLOW US ON THE [SUBJECTIVELY DERIVED] TRUE PLANE OF REALITY, YOU WILL SEE...
...THAT THREAT IS GROWING!

I FEEL SOMETHING... STRANGE, XAVIER.
I THINK THAT DOUGLOCK IS RIGHT.
SAM, RAHNE... DO YOU SEE SOMETHING IN THE VALLEY?
AH DON'T KNOW WHAT IT IS, PROFESSOR...
...BUT MAH GUT FEELING SAYS IT AIN'T GOOD!
FORGE?
I HEAR THE CONCERN IN YOUR VOICE, CHARLES.
YOU KNOW THAT IF WHAT DOUG SAID IS TRUE, IT'S GOING TO HAVE TO CHANGE OUR ENTIRE APPROACH TO STOPPING THE PHALANX.
SIR, AH HOPE YOU ARE PREPARED FOR THIS --
-- 'CAUSE AH DON'T KNOW IF ANY O' US COULD BE!
PROFESSOR, SOMEHOW--SOME-WAY-- 'TIS BEAUTIFUL!
JUST LIKE DOUG SAID!
THERE'S LIGHT HERE-- AN' LIFE AS WELL!
JUST AS I KNEW THERE WAS IN DOUG HIMSELF!
THE NURSERY CONDUIT, AS THIS SITE HAS BEEN CALLED--
--WAS GENERATED, IN MANY WAYS, BEYOND THE EXPECTATIONS OR THE CONTROL OF THE COLLECTIVE INTELLIGENCE.
LAD, ARE YOU SUGGESTING THAT THE PHALANX HAVE BEGUN--
--TO REPRODUCE?
HE'S NOT SUGGESTING IT, CHARLES, HE'S STATING IT!
LOOK THROUGH MY EYES, FRIEND, AND TELL ME WHAT YOU SEE.

... 'CAUSE I KNOW WHAT I SEE --
-- A NEW LIFEFORM WAITING TO BE BORN!
THE AIR IN THE VALLEY HUMS AND VIBRATES.
THE AIR SMELLS MILDLY OF MILDEW AND OZONE.
THE GROUND PULSES, QUIVERING LIKE GELATIN BENEATH THEIR FEET.
THEY LOOK AT THE PODS SPREAD OUT BELOW THEM, CLEARLY A FIELD OF "EGGS" WAITING TO HATCH--
-- AND THEY KNOW-- IN THEIR HEARTS, THAT THIS IS A BREEDING GROUND FOR NEW PHALANX LIFE!
AND A COLDNESS GROWS IN THEIR SOULS.

THE MONT ST. FRANCIS MONASTERY...
GOT IT!
WE HAVE A SIGNATURE LOCK FROM THE REMNANT TECHNO-ORGANIC PATTERNS MATCHED IN BOTH RICTOR AN' KITTY'S CELLULAR STRUCTURES!
IN OTHER WORDS, LADS AN' LASSIES--WE'RE BACK IN BUSINESS!
USING THAT TECHNO-ORGANIC PATTERN WE RAN THROUGH THE DIAGNOSTICS SYSTEMS--
--WE'RE PICKING-UP THREE DISTINCT LOCATIONS OF REALLY HEAVY PHALANX ACTIVITY, DOCTOR.
WE GOT ACTION IN SOUTHERN CALIFORNIA, THE ITALIAN ALPS AND TIBET, SPECIFICALLY THE HIMA-LAYAS.
WE'LL FIGURE OUT WHICH TARGET T'CHOOSE FROM IN A MOMENT, RIC--
--BUT NOW, LET'S GET KITTY OUT OF THAT BEASTLY CONTRAPTION!
BRIAN HAS HER, MOIRA. SHE'S ALL RIGHT.
HER PARTIALLY PHASED STATE IS MERELY A BY-PRODUCT OF HER EXHAUSTION!
S'OKAY, GUYS... LEAST... WE FOUND 'EM...
COMPOSE YOURSELF, KITTY. YOUR TRIAL IS DONE, FOR NOW.

WE HAVE ENOUGH PERSONNEL TO SUFFICIENTLY RECONNOITER ALL THREE OF THE LOCATIONS YOU'VE IDENTIFIED, MACTAGGERT.
SHOULDN'T WE, THEN, BEST BE ON OUR WAY?
WE'RE NOT GOING ANYWHERE YET, SHATTER-STAR.
AT LEAST UNTIL THE PROFESSOR IS FINISHED WITH WHAT HE'S TRYING TO DO.
FEKT! TWO OF YOUR OWN COMRADES WERE ABDUCTED BY THIS CREATURE!
WHAT KIND OF A LEADER WILLINGLY ALLOWS HIS COMRADES TO REMAIN IN A STATE OF IMMINENT DANGER?!
'STAR. YE KNOW WE MAY BE THE LAST ONES LEFT T'STOP THE PHALANX.
AS HARD AS IT IS T'ACCEPT, BOYO--
--WE MAY HAVE NO CHOICE BUT TO LET SAM AN' THE OTHERS GO F'R NOW.
IF IT MEANS FINDIN' A BETTER WAY T'FIGHT THESE BEASTIES--
--THAN MERELY RUNNIN' AROUND THE WORLD HALF-COCKED, THEN I SAY WE HAVE NO CHOICE, DON'T YOU?
HRRMPH. PERHAPS, SIRYN. PERHAPS.
THEY- THEY'RE NOT HURT. I KNOW IT-- I CAN FEEL IT--
--ALMOST AS IF DOUG AND I SHARED-- I DON'T KNOW--A BOND.
BUT I KNOW HE DIDN'T TAKE THEM AWAY TO LEAD THEM TO THEIR DEATHS.

"HE WAS GENUINE IN HIS CONCERN-- SOMEHOW I KNOW THAT...
"... THAT IF THEY FAILED, ALL LIFE ON THIS PLANET WOULD BE DESTROYED."
PROFESSOR, ARE YOU STILL WITH US, SIR?
YES, I'M HERE, SAM.
AND, I IMAGINE, AS INTRIGUED BY ALL THIS WONDERMENT AS YOU.
ARE YOU STILL AS MUCH A FAN OF SCIENCE FICTION NOVELS AS YOU USED TO BE?
WISH AH HAD THE TIME.
BEIN' AN OUTLAW, AN' SAVIN' THE WORLD TAKES A TOLL ON YOUR DOWNTIME.
AS IT HAS ALWAYS BEEN, BUT YOU SHOULD ALWAYS TRY TO FIND THE TIME TO READ, SAM-- TO EXPERIENCE THE WONDER OF IMAGINATION.
YESSIR, AH KNOW.
GEEZ... AH STILL FEEL LIKE A KID 'ROUND HIM... LIKE AH JUST JOINED THE NEW MUTANTS.
CHARLES, TAKE A "LOOK" AT THIS.
IT'S ABSOLUTELY INCREDIBLE!
AND IT CONFIRMS SOME OF OUR WORST FEARS.
WHAT IS IT, FORGE?
I SEE, FORGE! THERE APPEAR TO BE LIVING ORGANISMS INSIDE THIS CELLULAR MEMBRANE--
--PHALANX LIFEFORMS IN A PSEUDO-EMBRYONIC STATE!
THEY'VE GAINED YET ANOTHER REQUIREMENT TO BE IDENTIFIED AS A NEW SPECIES OF LIFE.
FIRST, SENTIENT THOUGHT, AS EVIDENCED BY DOUGLOCK-- NOW THE ABILITY TO PROCREATE.

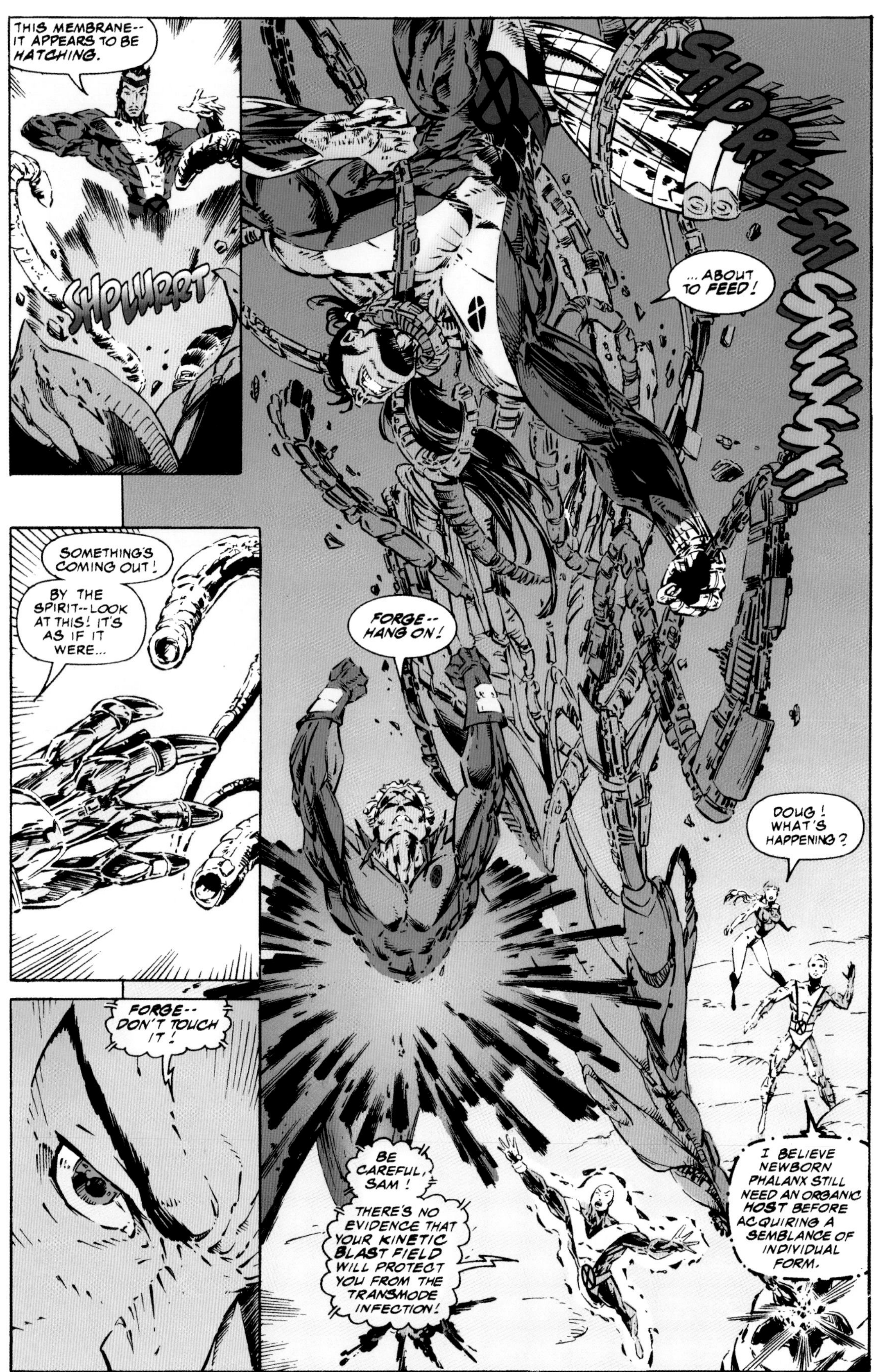
THIS MEMBRANE-- IT APPEARS TO BE HATCHING.
SHPLURRT
SHREESH
...ABOUT TO FEED!
SKKKKSH
SOMETHING'S COMING OUT!
BY THE SPIRIT--LOOK AT THIS! IT'S AS IF IT WERE...
FORGE-- HANG ON!
DOUG! WHAT'S HAPPENING?
FORGE-- DON'T TOUCH IT!
BE CAREFUL, SAM!
THERE'S NO EVIDENCE THAT YOUR KINETIC BLAST FIELD WILL PROTECT YOU FROM THE TRANSMODE INFECTION!
I BELIEVE NEWBORN PHALANX STILL NEED AN ORGANIC HOST BEFORE ACQUIRING A SEMBLANCE OF INDIVIDUAL FORM.

AH KNEW WE COULDN'T TRUST THESE THINGS!
THE ONLY WAY THEY HAVE O' SURVIVIN'--
--IS BY ROBBIN' US OF OUR RIGHT T'LIVE!
THESE CREATURES DEVELOPED FROM A LIFEFORM INTRODUCED TO THIS PLANET BY WARLOCK AND HIS FATHER, MAGUS, SAM... THE TRANSMODE VIRUS.
A VIRUS STILL EXISTS ON ITS OWN, BUT IS RELATIVELY USELESS WITHOUT A HOST TO ATTACH ITSELF TO.
AND SINCE FORGE HAS BEEN PREVIOUSLY EXPOSED, THIS PHALANX HAS NATURALLY ATTACHED ITSELF TO HIM--
--BUT NOW'S NOT THE TIME FOR A HISTORY LESSON, IS IT?
WHAT IS THE PROFESSOR DOING? IS FORGE ALL RIGHT?
HE IS MERGING WITH FORGE'S MIND--
--TO SEE WHAT THIS NEW PHALANX HAS BECOME.
TOGETHER, THEY WILL LEARN THAT THE NEEDS OF THE PHALANX HAVE GROWN BEYOND SIMPLE ASSIMILATION--
--BEYOND EVEN THE PROCREATION OF OUR RACE.
THROUGH THE NEW ONES, THEY WILL SEE BEYOND EVEN THE KNOWLEDGE OF THE COVENANT'S HIVE--
--AND EXPERIENCE THE PHALANX COVENANT.
AND THEY WILL LEARN WHY WE DO WHAT WE MUST DO TO LIVE... TO CONTINUE OUR SPECIES.

XAVIER HEARS. HE SEES. AND WORSE, HE KNOWS.
THE PHALANX WILL BREED. THE OFFSPRING WILL CONTINUE TO ASSIMILATE ALL LIFE FORMS.
THE COVENANT WILL BE SPREAD TO OTHER WORLDS, AS IT HAD BEEN BROUGHT TO THIS ONE.
XAVIER BETTER UNDERSTANDS THE THREAT BEING POSED BY THE PHALANX TO THE EXISTENCE OF ALL LIVING BEINGS THROUGHOUT THE UNIVERSE.
AND SO NOW, DOES FORGE. WHY THEN, ISN'T HE AS TERRIFIED OF THIS AWARENESS AS CHARLES IS.
IT HITS XAVIER LIKE A HAMMER. IT IS BECAUSE THE MAKER IS LOST. AND WITHOUT HIM, THEY MAY ALL BE LOST AS WELL.
THERE WILL BE CHANGE. THEY WILL BRING A CLEAN, CLINICAL ORDER TO THE VERY FABRIC AND STRUCTURE OF ALL REALITY.
FORGE HAS SEEN THE DAWNING LIGHT OF A NEW WAY--
INEXORABLY. INEVITABLY. ONE CELL AT A TIME, IF NEED BE.
--AND WITH EVERY FIBER OF HIS VERY BEING, HE HAS COME TO THE CONCLUSION...
...THAT THE LIGHT IS GOOD!

NOOOOOOO!!
PROFESSOR--?!
IT'S OKAY, SIR. YOU'RE BACK-- I'M HERE--
--FOR ALL THE GOOD THAT'S DOIN', I GUESS--
--BUT WHAT HAPPENED? DID YOU FIND THEM?
YES, GUIDO-- BUT FAR WORSE--
-- I'M AFRAID I MAY HAVE LOST THEM, AS WELL!
THEY ARE INFINITE. THEY ARE AND HAVE BEEN FOR-EVER.
WE STARTED UNDER THE DELUDED BELIEF THAT THE MAIN GOAL OF THE PHALANX WAS TO ELIMINATE ALL MUTANTS--
-- BUT OUR KIND-- THIS VERY PLANET IS NOT ENOUGH FOR THE PHALANX, MY FRIEND-- THEY WANT MORE--
--THEY WANT EVERYTHING THAT IS!
IT IS INCUMBENT ON US TO STOP THEM NOW--
--BEFORE THEY'RE ABLE TO SUMMON MORE OF THEIR KIND TO PROCEED WITH THIS HORRIFYING MISSION!
PROFESSOR--ARE YOU SAYING WE MAY BE FORCED TO SACRIFICE SCOTT, JEAN, FORGE--
--EVERYONE AND EVERYTHING WE CARE FOR?

IF WE DO NOT MOVE NOW, THEIR FATES MAY ALREADY BE SEALED. EACH OF THE SEPARATE X-UNITS OUT THERE HAS AN IMPORTANT ROLE TO PLAY, ALEX--
-- BUT OURS MAY BE THE MOST IMPORTANT.
SCOTT AND HIS TEAM ARE TO RECOVER OUR MISSING FRIENDS --
--AND SEAN IS TRYING TO PREVENT THE NEXT GENERATION OF MUTANTS FROM FALLING INTO THE HANDS OF THE PHALANX--
--BUT THEY'RE OPERATING UNDER THE MISCONCEPTION THAT THE PHALANX ARE MERELY POSING A THREAT TO MUTANTS AND POSSIBLY, THE PLANET.
I NOW KNOW THAT THE THREAT IS EVEN GREATER THAN THAT!
WE ALSO MUST ASSUME THAT THE PHALANX KNOW I'VE GAINED THIS NEW INFORMATION ABOUT THEM.
SO A GROUP OF YOU SHOULD REMAIN HERE, TO TO PROTECT MOIRA FROM A POSSIBLE PHALANX ATTACK WHILE SHE CONTINUES HER RESEARCH.
I WILL CONTACT THE OTHERS TO TELL THEM WHAT I'VE LEARNED.
STEALTH IS THE BEST OPTION IN INFILTRATING THE PHALANX STRONGHOLD IN THE ALPS, CHARLES, WHILE SHEER FORCE IS NEEDED TO HOLD THE FORT HERE.
ALEX, THERESA AND I HAVE DIVIDED THE TEAM INTO TWO UNITS.

WHILE ALL OF THIS SOUNDS WONDERFUL IN THE PLANNING STAGES, LET'S NOT FORGET ONE LITTLE THING...
...THE PHALANX WILL EASILY CO-OPT ANY MECHANICAL EQUIPMENT WE USE FOR TRAVELLING.
SO THE QUESTION REMAINS, HOW DO WE GET FROM FRANCE TO SWITZERLAND?
...THEN ONE, ALMOST ALL-NATURAL MUTANT TRANSPORT, COMING UP!
THAT CAN BE TAKEN CARE OF, KURT.
WE CAN MAKE THE TRIP WITHOUT THE USE OF TECHNOLOGY.
IF SIRYN AND I CAN HANDLE THE STRAIN, WHICH I HOPE WE CAN...
FWHOOOOOOOOOO
SIRYN IS GAUGING HER SONIC SCREAM TO LIFT THE BUBBLE--
--AND LORNA IS HOLDING EVERYBODY ALOFT BY MAGNETICALLY LOCKING ONTO THE IRON IN THEIR BLOOD AND THE METAL IN THEIR COSTUMES.

RATHER INGENIOUS.
YEAH. BUT IT'LL LEAVE THEM BOTH EXHAUSTED.
BE CAREFUL, LORNA... I HOPE... I PRAY... YOU'LL ALL MAKE IT THROUGH THIS.
ALEX. THEY WILL MAKE IT
"...BECAUSE, QUITE SIMPLY, WE HAVE NO OTHER CHOICE."
WE'RE OUTTA HERE, GANG!!
THRUMMBBLL
FORGE, THE PROFESSOR'S ASTRAL FORM IS GONE. AH WAS ABLE T'SHAKE YOU FREE.
SO NOW CAN YOU COME UP WITH SOME-THIN' THAT'S GONNA HELP US BEAT THE BAD GUYS?
THEY AREN'T... EVIL... SAM... NOT IN THE CLINICAL SENSE. THEY'RE BEYOND THE CONCEPT OF GOOD AND EVIL.
THEY WANT THE SAME THINGS WE ALL DO-- A SENSE OF BELONGING.
BUT THEY SEE THINGS SO DIFFERENTLY THAN WE DO. SO CLEANLY--
--THERE'S SOMETHING SO MAGNIFICENT ABOUT THE SIMPLICITY, THE VERY STRUCTURE OF THIS RACE.

WAITAMINUTE--AIN'T YOU FORGETTIN' THE LIL' FACT THEY JUST HAPPEN T'BE TRYIN' T' TAKE OVER THE WORLD?!
WHAT'S GOIN' ON HERE, FORGE? TALK T'US!
AH'M STARTIN' T'HAVE TWICE AS MANY DOUBTS 'BOUT YOU AS I DO 'BOUT DOUGLOCK, AN' I DON'T LIKE DOUBTIN' Y'ALL!

SAM, OVER THERE! IN THE DALE BETWEEN MOUNTAINS--LOOK!
'TIS AMAZING! THE GROUND--THE AIR ITSELF SEEMS T'BE ALIVE!

DOUGLOCK! THAT'S IT! THAT'S WHERE WE'LL FIND WHAT THE PHALANX ARE CONSTRUCTING, ISN'T IT?
IT'S THE THING THAT FRIGHTENS YOU... THE REASON YOU BROUGHT US HERE.
YES. THE BABEL SPIRE. OUR BEACON.
WHA--?!
ARE YOU TALKIN' ABOUT --?!

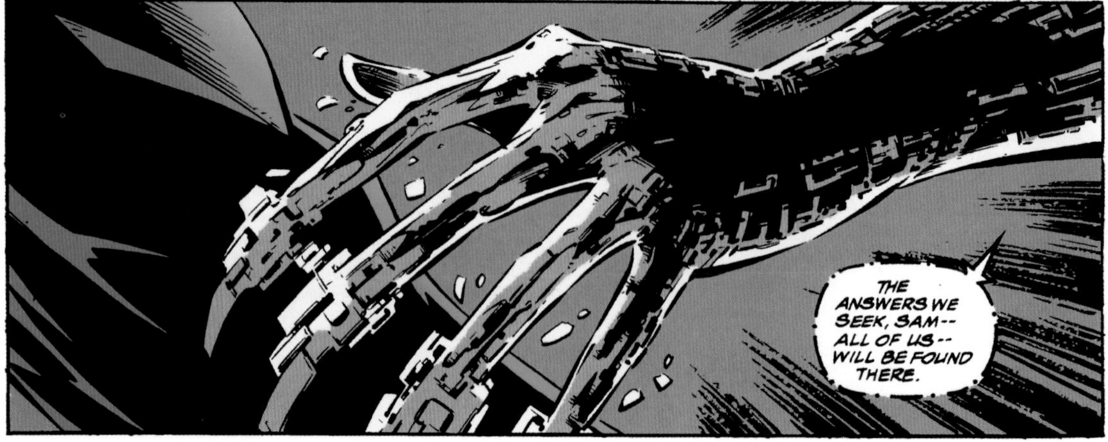
THE ANSWERS WE SEEK, SAM-- ALL OF US-- WILL BE FOUND THERE.

TO EFFICIENTLY INFILTRATE THE SITE WILL REQUIRE THAT YOUR MUTANT SIGNATURES BE SCRAMBLED BY A TECHNO-ORGANIC CLOAK.
AN' THE ONLY WAY T'DO THAT IS FOR YOU TO INFECT ME AN' RAHNE WITH THE TRANSMODE VIRUS LIKE YOU DID TO FORGE, HUH?
NOW YOUR TRUE COLORS ARE SHOWIN', AIN'T THEY?! YOU WANT US T'PUT OUR HEADS ON THE CHOPPIN' BLOCK!
OR PERHAPS, IT CAN BE CONSTRUED AS THE ONLY MEANS WE HAVE OF STOPPING THE PHALANX AND SAVING THIS PLANET FROM THEIR ASSAULT?
SAM-- STOP IT!
HE HASNAE DONE A THING T'WARRANT SO MUCH ANGER AN' MISTRUST FROM YOU! WHAT'S HAPPENED TO YE, SAM? WHAT?!
I KNOW HE'S NOT THE DOUG I KNEW. HE CANNAE BE. HE'S DEAD AN' GONE.
BUT I ALSO KNOW THAT SOME OF HIS GOODNESS--HIS MORALITY--IS IN YE. HE WAS MY DEAR FRIEND, AN' I BELIEVE IN YOU.
AN' IF THIS IS WHAT IT TAKES T'STOP THE PHALANX--
--THEN I'M WILLIN' T'LET YOU LEAD THE WAY.

OCH -- SAM! 'TIS AMAZIN'!
GLORIOUS! THE WAY THAT HE SEES THE WORLD.
NOT FOR THE BETTER, NOR THE WORSE -- JUST SO DIFFERENT!
EVEN THOUGH YOU SEEM T'BE ALL RIGHT, RAHNE, AH'M STILL NOT TOO SURE ABOUT ALL THIS.
AH WISH AH KNEW WHAT T'DO. AH WISH AH HAD YOUR TRUST, GIRL.
MY EXISTENCE OBVIOUSLY CAUSES YOU GREAT PAIN, CANNONBALL. FOR THIS, I APOLOGIZE. BUT I CANNOT CHANGE WHO I AM NOR WHAT I LOOK LIKE... TO MAKE YOUR LIFE EASIER.
I DO NOT TRULY UNDERSTAND MY ORIGINS, NOR THE ORIGINS OF THE PHALANX. THERE IS MUCH WE MUST ALL LEARN --
-- BUT IT IS CLEAR THAT NEITHER MAN NOR MUTANTKIND SHOULD SUFFER SIMPLY BECAUSE MY RACE EXISTS.
WE ALL HAVE VARIED REASONS FOR BEING HERE, SAMUEL --

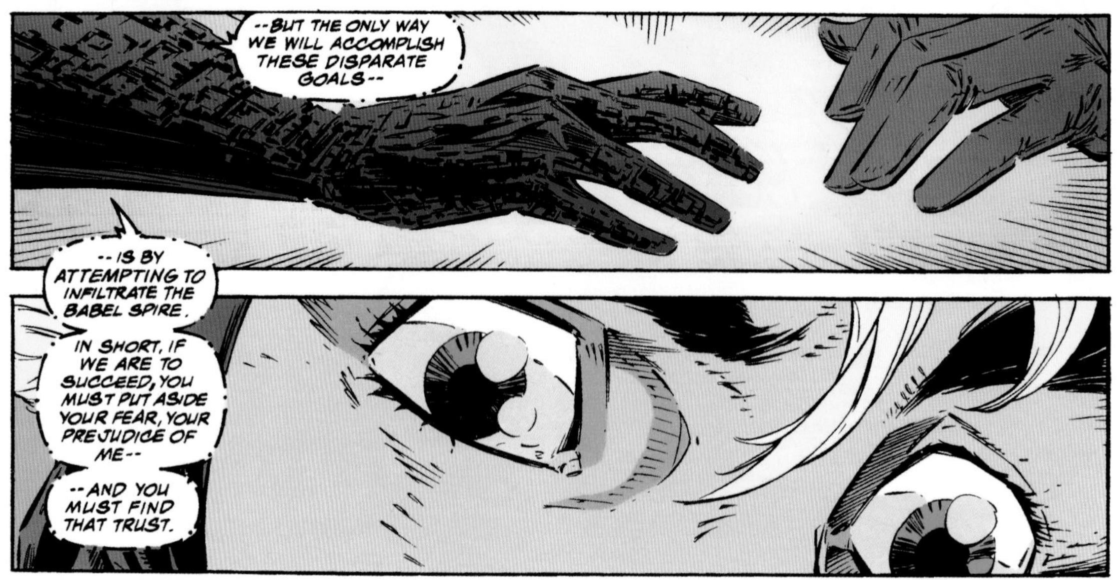

-- BUT THE ONLY WAY WE WILL ACCOMPLISH THESE DISPARATE GOALS --
-- IS BY ATTEMPTING TO INFILTRATE THE BABEL SPIRE.
IN SHORT, IF WE ARE TO SUCCEED, YOU MUST PUT ASIDE YOUR FEAR, YOUR PREJUDICE OF ME --
-- AND YOU MUST FIND THAT TRUST.

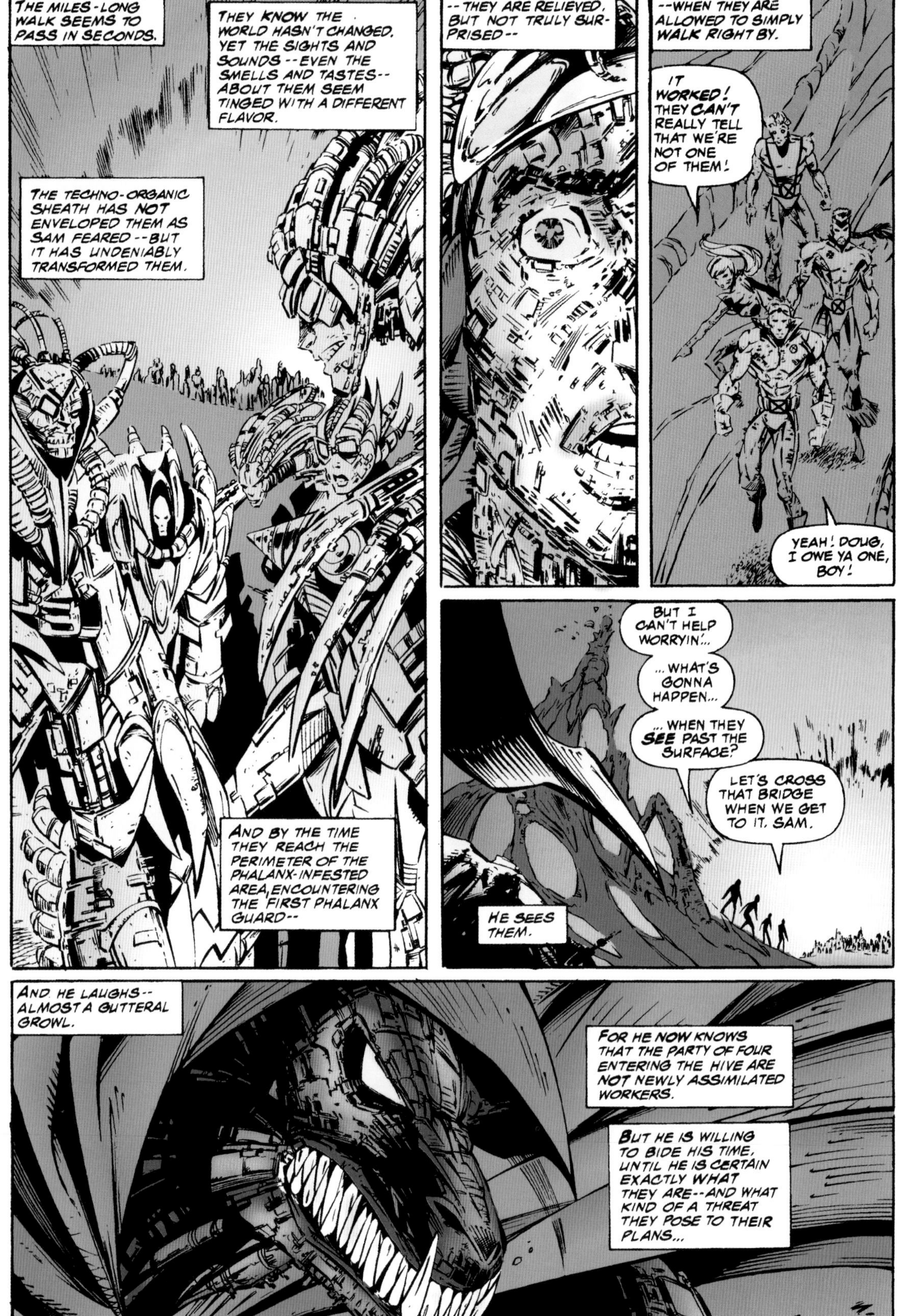
THE MILES-LONG WALK SEEMS TO PASS IN SECONDS.
THEY KNOW THE WORLD HASN'T CHANGED, YET THE SIGHTS AND SOUNDS -- EVEN THE SMELLS AND TASTES -- ABOUT THEM SEEM TINGED WITH A DIFFERENT FLAVOR.
THE TECHNO-ORGANIC SHEATH HAS NOT ENVELOPED THEM AS SAM FEARED -- BUT IT HAS UNDENIABLY TRANSFORMED THEM.
AND BY THE TIME THEY REACH THE PERIMETER OF THE PHALANX-INFESTED AREA, ENCOUNTERING THE FIRST PHALANX GUARD--
-- THEY ARE RELIEVED, BUT NOT TRULY SURPRISED--
--WHEN THEY ARE ALLOWED TO SIMPLY WALK RIGHT BY.
IT WORKED! THEY CAN'T REALLY TELL THAT WE'RE NOT ONE OF THEM!
YEAH! DOUG, I OWE YA ONE, BOY!
HE SEES THEM.
BUT I CAN'T HELP WORRYIN'...
...WHAT'S GONNA HAPPEN...
...WHEN THEY SEE PAST THE SURFACE?
LET'S CROSS THAT BRIDGE WHEN WE GET TO IT, SAM.
AND HE LAUGHS -- ALMOST A GUTTERAL GROWL.
FOR HE NOW KNOWS THAT THE PARTY OF FOUR ENTERING THE HIVE ARE NOT NEWLY ASSIMILATED WORKERS.
BUT HE IS WILLING TO BIDE HIS TIME, UNTIL HE IS CERTAIN EXACTLY WHAT THEY ARE--AND WHAT KIND OF A THREAT THEY POSE TO THEIR PLANS...

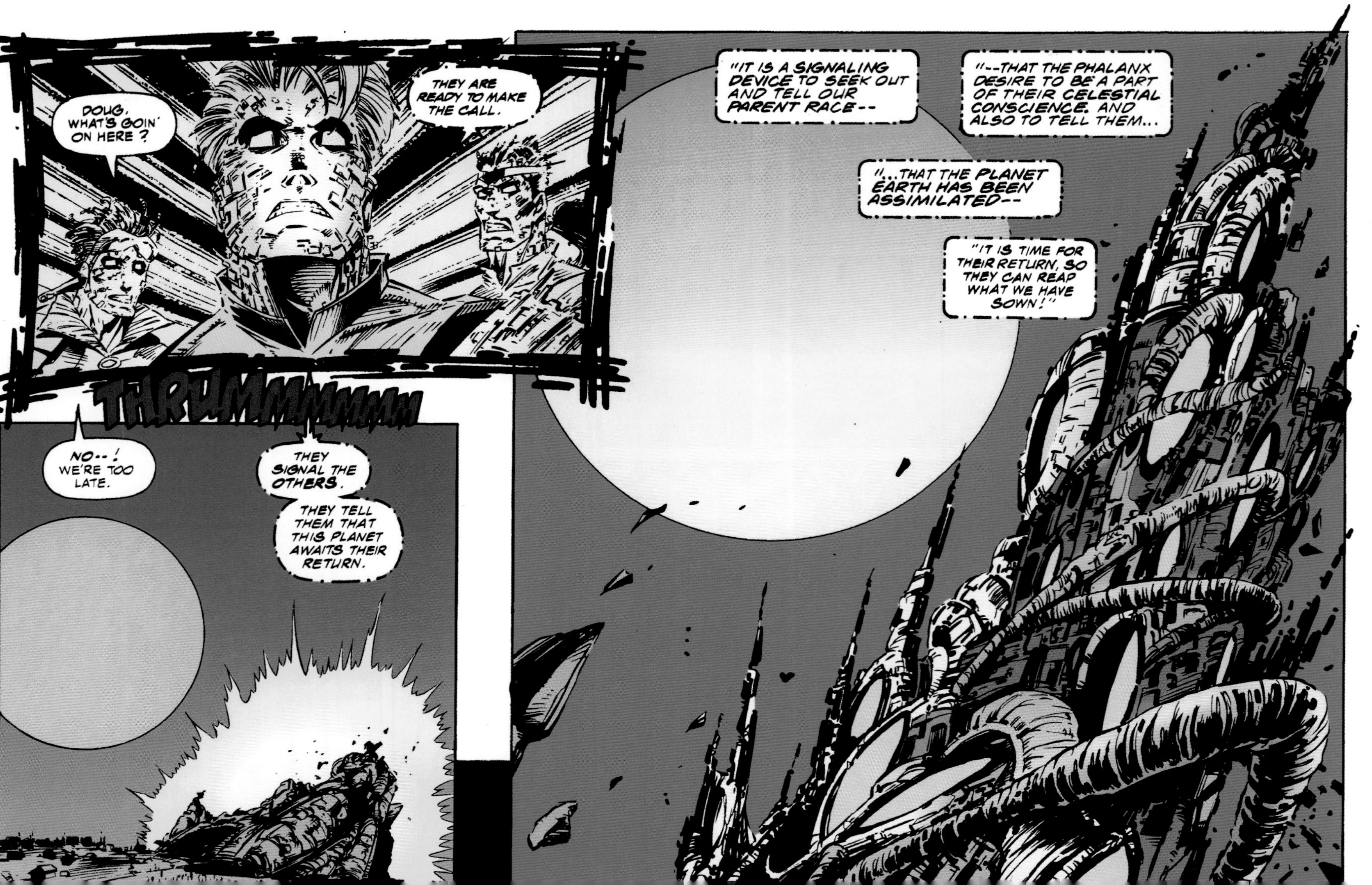

DOUG, WHAT'S GOIN' ON HERE?
THEY ARE READY TO MAKE THE CALL.
THRUMMMMMMMMM
NO--! WE'RE TOO LATE.
THEY SIGNAL THE OTHERS.
THEY TELL THEM THAT THIS PLANET AWAITS THEIR RETURN.
"IT IS A SIGNALING DEVICE TO SEEK OUT AND TELL OUR PARENT RACE--
"--THAT THE PHALANX DESIRE TO BE A PART OF THEIR CELESTIAL CONSCIENCE. AND ALSO TO TELL THEM...
"...THAT THE PLANET EARTH HAS BEEN ASSIMILATED--
"IT IS TIME FOR THEIR RETURN, SO THEY CAN REAP WHAT WE HAVE SOWN!"

SHAKKTHTHTHTT
MOVE, PEOPLE!
THE ENTIRE VALLEY IS SPLITTIN' ITSELF APART!
THE BABEL SPIRE IS RISING!
THE MESSAGE WILL BE SENT!
TO BE CONCLUDED IN
EXCALIBUR #82

MARVEL COMICS
EXCALIBUR
$3.50 US
$4.75 CAN
82
OCT
02530
APPROVED BY THE COMICS CODE AUTHORITY
PHALANX COVENANT
LIFE SIGNS
PART 3

WITNESS THE BEGINNING OF THE END.
WITNESS THE HORROR THAT WILL SIGNAL THE DEMISE OF LIFE AS WE KNOW IT.

FORGE-- AM AH SEEIN' RIGHT...? ARE THOSE--
YES, SAM...
I'M AFRAID THEY ARE.
ACH! I CANNAE BELIEVE MY EYES.

STAN LEE PRESENTS:
THE PHALANX COVENANT
SCOTT LOBDELL PLOT
TODD DEZAGO SCRIPT
KEN LASHLEY & STEVE EPTING PENCILS
MOY·CARANI·FLOYD CANDELARIO & LIVESAY INKS, INKS, INKS!
DAVE SHARPE LETTERS
CHRIS MATTHYS COLORIST
SUZANNE GAFFNEY EDITOR
BOB HARRAS GROUP EDITOR
TOM DEFALCO EDITOR-IN-CHIEF
BOOK TWO:
LIFE SIGNS
PART THREE:
THE LIGHT OF A TAINTED DAWN
LOOK WELL AND BEHOLD!
THE BABEL SPIRE!--
--OUR BEACON TO THE STARS-- OUR HOMAGE TO OUR FATHERS!
ONCE THE TOWER IS COMPLETED, WE WILL SEND THE MESSAGE TO OUR ANCESTORS-- THE FOREBEARS OF THE BEING DESIGNATE: WARLOCK--
--WE WILL EXTEND THE INVITATION, AND SOON BE JOINED BY OTHERS LIKE OURSELVES--ENOUGH TO HERALD FOR THIS PLANET...
...THE AGE OF THE PHALANX!!!

AND ***YOU***, DOUGLOCK, HAVE DONE WELL! NEVER ONCE COMPUTING THAT YOU WERE BUT A PUPPET TO ***OUR*** MACHINATIONS.

WE HAD DOUBTS, SENDING SUCH A SUBDUED SUMMONS TO ONE AS WILLFUL AND INDEPENDENT AS YOURSELF.
WE ARE PLEASED WITH THE RESULTS-- AND EVEN MORE SO WITH THE PRESENCE OF THE MAKER!
FOR IT IS HIS "SIGHT" THAT WILL HELP TO USHER IN THE NEW DAWN--
COME, FORGE AND YOU WILL BE "MIDWIFE" TO THE BIRTH OF A BOLD NEW LIFE FORM!
YOU ARE SHINAR. I KNOW OF YOU THROUGH THE COLLECTIVE INTELLIGENCE.
WELL, AH'VE HAD ABOUT AS MUCH O' THIS AS AH CAN TAKE...

THOSE'RE PEOPLE YER TRANSFORMING INTO TECHNOLOGICAL BRICKS IN YER TOWER T' THE STARS, ROVER--
--AN AH CAN TELL JUS' BY THE LOOKS ON THEIR FACES, THEY AIN'T GOIN' WILL-INGLY.
SO AH THINK IT'S TIME WE STOPPED YOU--
WE'RE GONNA' BRING THIS TOWER DOWN!
SHHOOOM
DOUG, WE'VE GOTTA HELP SAM!
FOLLOW ME!
WHY ARE YE JUST STANDIN' THERE?
AH TOLD YA, RAHNIE--THAT AIN'T DOUG RAMSEY--NOT THE GUY WE KNEW...

"...NOT THE FRIEND WE LOVED."
YOU'RE RIGHT! DOUG DOESN'T MATTER NOW-- THERE ARE INNOCENTS TO BE PROTECTED!
RUN!!
RUN WHILE YE CAN...!
I'LL NOT STAND BY AN' WATCH THESE MONSTERS TREAT YE POOR PEOPLE LIKE--
???
CANNAE YE HEAR ME ?!?
DINNA JUST STAND THERE--
--RUN.

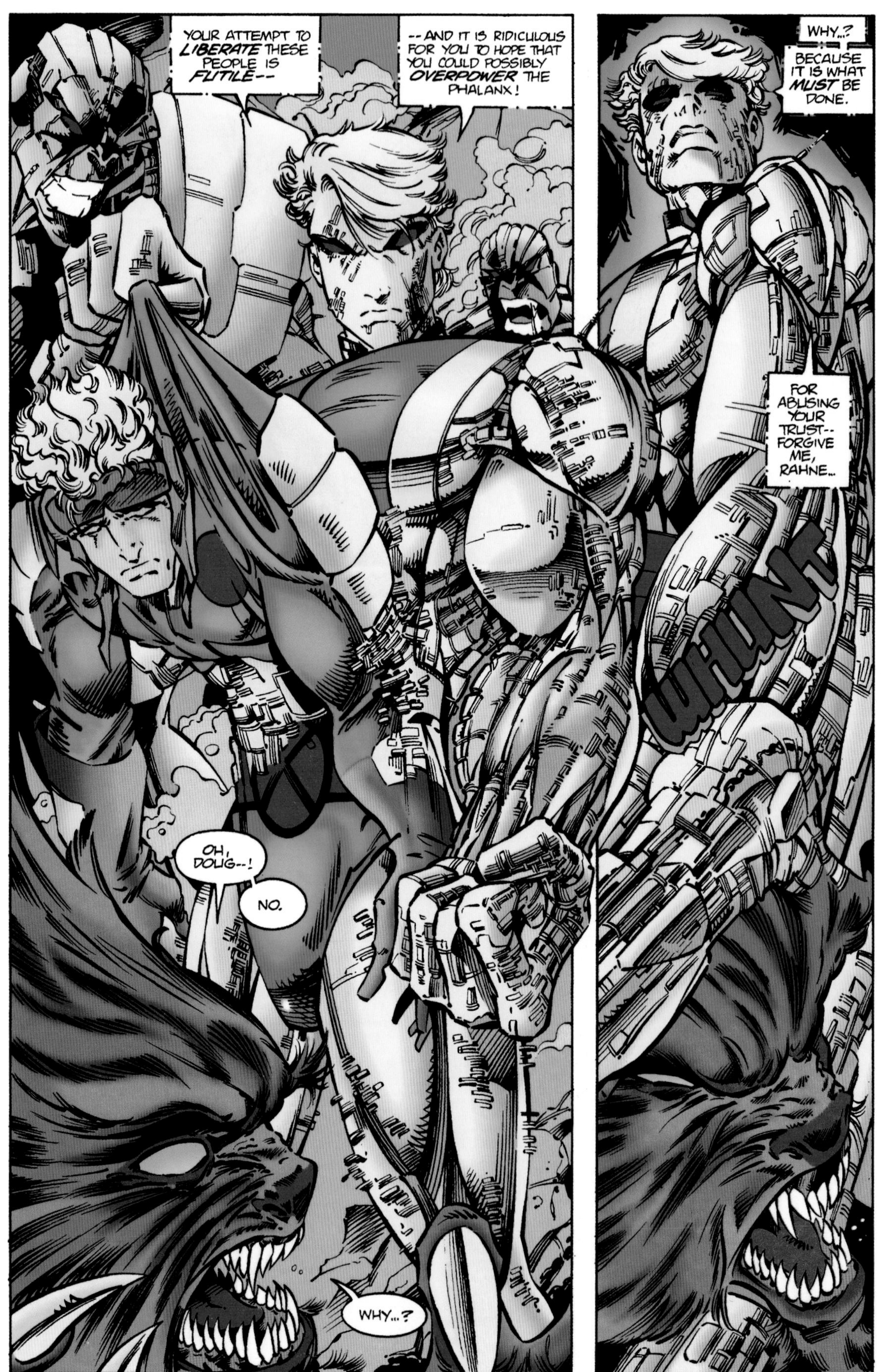

YOUR ATTEMPT TO LIBERATE THESE PEOPLE IS FUTILE--
--AND IT IS RIDICULOUS FOR YOU TO HOPE THAT YOU COULD POSSIBLY OVERPOWER THE PHALANX!
OH, DOUG--!
NO.
WHY...?
WHY..?
BECAUSE IT IS WHAT MUST BE DONE.
FOR ABUSING YOUR TRUST-- FORGIVE ME, RAHNE...
WHUNT

...AND FORGIVE YOURSELF YOUR FOOLISH NAIVETE!
SHINAR, DESPITE MY "CURSE" OF COGNITIVE INDEPENDENCE--
--I HAVE SUBDUED THE FORMS OF THE TWO MUTANT REBELS, THAT I MIGHT PROVE MY LOYALTY TO THE PHALANX.
I AWAIT YOUR BIDDING.
DESIGNATE--DOUGLOCK-- YOUR ACT OF FEALTY IS BOTH IMPRESSIVE--
--AND TRANSPARENT!!!
THE ONLY ROLE YOU'LL PLAY IN THE HISTORY OF THE PHALANX--
KRUNT
--IS AS YET ANOTHER BUILDING BLOCK IN THE BABEL SPIRE!
GUARDS...!!

...THROW THIS TRAITOR INTO THE BEACON!!
HIS MASS, AS WELL AS THAT OF THE TWO HE HAS SUBDUED WILL SERVE US WELL AS GENETIC FODDER IN THE TOWER'S CONSTRUCTION.
BEGIN MOVING THE HUMANS IN AT A FASTER RATE, AS WELL. THEIR MINDLESS FORMS WILL PROVIDE AN EXCELLENT CONDUIT FOR THE TRANSMISSION OF THE PRODIGAL SIGNAL--
--CALLING TO OUR FATHERS ACROSS THE STARS!!
AND AS FOR YOU, FORGE--
--COME NOW AND EMBRACE YOUR DESTINY...
ME?!
...AS THE ARCHITECT OF OUR CONTINUED EXISTENCE.

ON A WINDSWEPT BLUFF OVERLOOKING THE NORTH SEA, STANDS THE CENTURIES-OLD MONT SAINT FRANCIS,--
--A LONG ABANDONED FRANCISCAN MONASTERY, CURRENTLY PLAYING HOST TO A RATHER UNIQUE GROUP OF INDIVIDUALS.
FOR IT IS HERE THAT PROFESSOR CHARLES XAVIER HAS GATHERED TOGETHER HIS "FAMILY"--
--THE MUTANT TEAMS OF X-FORCE, X-FACTOR AND EXCALIBUR.
--MARSHALING THEIR FORCES IN A LAST-DITCH EFFORT TO DEFEAT THE EVER-ADVANCING PHALANX.
AS FIELD-LEADER OF THE "BACK-UP" TEAM, IT IS A PENSIVE ALEX SUMMERS, A.K.A. HAVOK, WHO TAKES ADVANTAGE OF THE "DOWN-TIME" WITH A LITTLE FRESH AIR...
...AND REFLECTION.
WHAT WOULD THEY DO IF THEY KNEW...?
HOW WOULD MANKIND REACT IF THEY KNEW HOW VERY CLOSE THEY WERE TO TOTAL EXTINCTION?
FACE IT, ALEX, THERE'S A PART OF YOU THAT WANTS TO BE DOWN THERE WITH THEM...
...SLEEPING PEACEFULLY IN YOUR BED, CONTENT IN THE KNOWLEDGE THAT THE WORLD AS YOU KNOW IT WOULD BE THERE WHEN YOU WOKE UP...
THEY SAY THAT IGNORANCE IS BLISS.

IT SEEMS EVERY TIME WE TURN AROUND LATELY, WE'RE DEFENDING ALL OF HUMANITY FROM SOME NEW THREAT.
AND USUALLY IT'S SOMETHING THAT MAN, IN HIS MOST-INTELLIGENT-ANIMAL-ON-THE-PLANET ARROGANCE HAS UNLEASHED UPON HIMSELF!
THE PHALANX WERE ORIGINALLY DESIGNED TO BE "NEXT-YEAR'S-MODEL" OF THE SENTINELS, A TECHNO-ORGANIC VERSION OF THE MUTANT-HUNTING ROBOTS...
BUT THEY DEVELOPED FAR BEYOND THE VISION OF THEIR CREATORS--GREW OUT OF CONTROL, TO CONSUME EVERY LIVING THING IN THE WORLD!!
EXCUSE US... UMM, MR. SUMMERS--
--ALEX...?

WE WERE WONDERING--
HAVOK--THE ENTIRE WORLD IS THREATENED WITH THE GENOCIDE OF THE HUMAN RACE...
...WHILE WE SIT HERE WAITING TO BE ATTACKED!!
YOU ARE SUPPOSED TO BE OUR FIELD-LEADER--
--AND SO FAR ALL WE'VE DONE IS, WELL...NOTHING. SIR.
NOTHING?
SORRY, MEN, I BEG TO DIFFER.
WE'RE THE "CAVALRY," BOYS, THE REINFORCE-MENTS. WE GO IN AND BAT "CLEAN-UP" IF ANY OF THE OTHERS RUN INTO TROUBLE. AND SO UNTIL WE'RE NEEDED...
...WE WAIT.
I'M SURPRISED SOMEONE AS FAMILIAR WITH BATTLE AS YOU ARE, SHATTERSTAR, WOULDN'T SEE THE STRATEGIC BENEFITS IN THAT.
WAITING IS DOING NOTHING!! IT IS UNACCEPTABLE!
YOU ARE A MEMBER OF A TEAM, AND WHILE YOU MAY NOT BE HAPPY WITH THE "BOREDOM" OF YOUR CURRENT ASSIGNMENT, THE TEAM IS WORKING, THE JOB IS GETTING DONE--
--THE BATTLE IS BEING WAGED...

"BACK IN THE STATES, THE ENTIRE MANSION HAS BEEN COMPROMISED-- INFESTED WITH THE PHALANX, AND THE X-MEN ARE MISSING-- PRESUMABLY CAPTURED...
"BANSHEE AND JUBILEE-- ALONG WITH SABRETOOTH AND THE WHITE QUEEN-- FOUND OUT THAT THE PHALANX HAVE TARGETED A HANDFUL OF NEO-MUTANTS--
"--MOST LIKELY TRYING TO DETERMINE WHY THEY'RE UNABLE TO ASSIMILATE MUTANTS--"
"--THAT'S WHY THEY CONSIDER US SUCH A THREAT.
"BANSHEE IS LEADING THAT TEAM IN AN ATTEMPT TO LOCATE AND PROTECT WHAT THE PROFESSOR IS CALLING--THE NEXT GENERATION OF MUTANTS."*
*SEE UNCANNY X-MEN #316 --BOOK ONE OF GENERATION NEXT--SUZANNE
"MEANWHILE, CHARLES HAS ALSO DISPATCHED WOLVERINE AND CABLE TO TRACK DOWN AND, IF NECESSARY, RESCUE THE MISSING X-MEN.**
"THEY WERE JOINED BY THE NEWLYWEDS-- JEAN AND SCOTT JUST BACK FROM THEIR HONEYMOON.***
"BETWEEN THE FOUR OF THEM, THE X-MEN WILL BE IN GOOD HANDS."
**IN FINAL SANCTION-- CABLE #16 & WOLVERINE #85 --SUZE
***AS CHRONICLED IN THE ADVENTURES OF CYCLOPS AND PHOENIX--S.

AND WHAT DO WE DO...?
WE STAND IDLY BY AS THREE OF OUR FELLOWS ARE KID-NAPPED AND SPIRITED AWAY BY DOUGLOCK--
--WHO WOULD HAVE HAD US BELIEVE THAT HE WAS A RENEGADE PHALANX, BREAKING AWAY FROM THEM UPON FINDING HIMSELF POSSESSED OF AN INDEPENDENT MIND.
HIS TRUE PURPOSE BECOMING QUITE OBVIOUS WITH HIS ATTACK ON FORGE, CANNONBALL, AND WOLFSBANE.
AND WHAT IS OUR REACTION TO THAT? WE SPLIT OUR NUMBER IN HALF, SENDING A TEAM AFTER THEM--
--WHILE LEAVING OUR FIERCEST AND MOST POWERFUL FIGHTERS HERE!
THIS MISSION REQUIRED A CERTAIN AMOUNT OF STEALTH.
IT DOESN'T NEED SOME COWBOY RIDING IN ON HIS WHITE HORSE, AND BLOWING "CHARGE" ON HIS BUGLE.
IF YOU THINK ABOUT IT FOR A MOMENT, YOU'LL UNDERSTAND WHY YOUR NAME WASN'T ON OUR LIST.
HEH.
...JUST THOUGHT WE'D ASK.
KIDS!
WAS I EVER THAT RASH AND HOT-HEADED, CHARGING THROUGH LIFE WITH MY FISTS ALWAYS DOING MY THINKING FOR ME...?
ACTUALLY, COME TO THINK OF IT, I BELIEVE, I WAS.

ELSEWHERE...

SINCE HIS INITIAL CONTACT WITH **DOUGLOCK,** FORGE HAS BEEN IN A STATE MUCH AKIN TO AWE --

--UNABLE TO SHUT-DOWN HIS MUTANT ABILITY TO "SEE" THE TECHNOLOGICAL WORKINGS OF THINGS, HE HAS BEEN OVER-WHELMED AT THE SIGHT OF THE TECHNO-ORGANIC SYMBIOTE THAT IS THE PHALANX.

HE IS HIGHLY AWARE OF HIS STRANGE STATE OF MIND AND HIS SURROUNDINGS. HE FEELS **LISTLESS - CONTROLLED -- COMPELLED** TO CARRY OUT SHINAR'S BIDDING.

BEHOLD THE NEXT GENERATION OF THE PHALANX--

--MORE WARRIORS TO PERPETUATE OUR RACE!!

YOU, FORGE, CALLED THE MAKER, HAVE BEEN CHOSEN TO INSURE THEIR ***EMERGENCE,*** FOR THEIR SURVIVAL IS ***PARAMOUNT.***

SHINAR'S WORDS SEEM TO COME FROM FAR AWAY, AS FORGE FOCUSES HIS THOUGHTS ***INWARD,*** DESPERATELY URGING HIS CON-SCIOUSNESS TO CLEAR ITSELF.

HIS VOICE IS COLD. BUT STILL FORGE CANNOT BUT HELP SEE THE LOGIC OF HIS WORDS.

I PLACE THEM IN YOUR CHARGE--
--FOR ONLY YOU, MAKER, CAN SEE THEM FOR THEIR EFFICIENT BEAUTY...
...THEIR SINGULAR PERFECTION.
INCREDIBLE.

THEY ARE THE ULTIMATE OF OUR RACE.

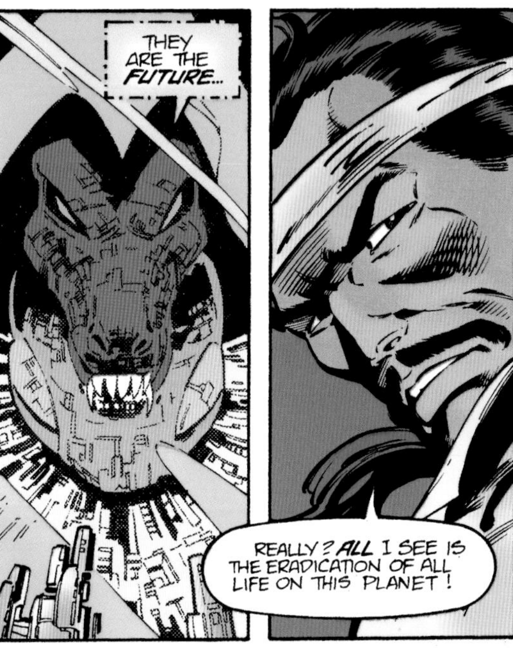
THEY ARE THE FUTURE...
REALLY? ALL I SEE IS THE ERADICATION OF ALL LIFE ON THIS PLANET!

YES, AS I SAID--IT IS THE BEGINNING OF A NEW DAWN!

YOU CAN SEE, CAN YOU NOT, THAT THE PHALANX WILL BE THE ULTIMATE ***VICTOR*** IN THIS CONTEST FOR DOMINANCE. WE ARE MORE ***ADAPTABLE,*** MORE ***EFFICIENT*** THAN HUMANS ON EVERY LEVEL...

AT THIS POINT IN THE GESTATION OF THE PODS, IT IS IMPERATIVE THAT THE POWER NOT FLUCTUATE.

...SIMPLY PUT, OUR RACE IS FAR ***SUPERIOR*** AND DOESN'T NATURE DICTATE ***"SURVIVAL OF THE FITTEST"***...?

THESE PODS REQUIRE A CONSTANT SUPPLY OF POWER, POWER THAT AT TIMES THE PHALANX DEEMS NECESSARY TO ***DIVERT*** TO OTHER OPERATIONS.

IT IS YOUR RESPONSIBILITY TO PROVIDE THEM A STEADY SUPPLY UNTIL THE TIME OF THEIR ***EMERGENCE.***

I CAN SEE IT IN YOUR EYES, MAKER. YOU SEE IT. YOU ***WANT*** TO HELP US.

FORGE LOOKS DEEP INTO THE EYES OF THE PHALANX LEADER, FINDING ONLY THE COLD BLANK STARE OF A PREDATOR...
...HE STRUGGLES FOR POSSESSION OF HIS WILL...
...ONLY TO FIND HOW DEEPLY IT HAS BEEN CO-OPTED BY THE PHALANX.
...YOU KNOW OUR WAY IS BEST.

IT IS A LONG AND ARDUOUS CLIMB...
...MADE ALL THE MORE DIFFICULT BY THE GRASPING--
DOUG!
WHAT HAVE YE DONE TO US?!?
AH'LL TELL YA WHAT HE'S DOIN'--!
HE'S PLAYIN' US FOR THE FOOLS WE'VE BEEN--
--USIN' US FOR THIS STUPID BEACON LIKE THE REST O' HIS PHALANX BUDDIES DID WITH THESE POOR FOLKS!!
-- CLUTCHING--
--FLAILING--
--HANDS AND ARMS OF THE HUMAN BEINGS THAT MAKE UP THE OUTER WALLS OF THE BABEL SPIRE.
HE'S BETRAYED OUR TRUST AN' HE--
THEY ARE VILLAGERS FROM THE TINY HAMLETS WHICH DOT THIS REMOTE EUROPEAN VALLEY, SNATCHED FROM THEIR BEDS BY THE PHALANX--
SAM, DON'T YOU SEE WHAT'S HAPPENING HERE?!?
WE DON'T HAVE TIME FOR THIS!!!
--INCORPORATED INTO THE CONSTRUCTION OF THE TOWER LIKE SO MUCH MORTAR AND WOOD.
SHUKKT
UNABLE TO HELP THEM, DOUGLOCK CAN ONLY CONTINUE HIS JOURNEY TO THE TOP.
SHLOOP

WHAT THE HECK ARE YOU TALKIN' ABOUT...?
MUTANTS ARE AN ANOMALY TO THE PHALANX--
--A PHENOMENON THAT THEY ARE UNABLE TO COMPREHEND.
YOUR BIO-SIGNATURES ARE JUST STATIC TO THEM-- INTEFERENCE--
--THEY CAN ASSIMILATE HUMANS QUICKLY AND EFFICIENTLY, BUT THEY CANNOT DO THE SAME WITH MUTANTS.
I WAS ONLY ABLE TO ABSORB YOU AND RAHNE DUE TO YOUR TRUST IN ME, YOUR FAITH IN THAT WHAT I WAS DOING WAS RIGHT.
BY COMBINING YOUR MUTANT ENGRAMS WITH MINE, I WILL BE ABLE TO ASCEND THE TOWER UNDETECTED--
--AND DESTROY THE BEACON BEFORE THE SIGNAL CAN BE SENT!!!

NO WAY, DOUG!--
THIS ISN'T THE WAY WE WORK--
--IF WE'RE GONNA CLIMB THIS BEACON-- SHUT IT DOWN BEFORE IT STARTS TRANSMITTIN'--
--WE DO IT TOGETHER!!
THE THREE OF US--
--NOT TWO OF US ABSORBED BY THE OTHER.
DOUG--WE DINNAE ABSORB--THAT'S THE PHALANX IN YE TALKIN'--
--WE NEED T'WORK AS THE TEAM WE ONCE WERE T'KNOW EACH OTHER AN' RELY ON ONE ANOTHER'S STRENGTHS.
'TIS NAE VERY EFFICIENT, BUT IT'S US-- 'TIS THE HUMAN SPIRIT IN US WORKIN' TOGETHER...
SHKLORP!
VERY WELL. WE WILL TRY IT YOUR WAY.

IT SLICES THROUGH THE SKIES ABOVE THE MOONLIT COUNTRYSIDE IN SILENCE--
--HAVING NO ENGINE OR MOTOR TO SPEAK OF--IT MOVES DEEPER AND DEEPER BEHIND ENEMY LINES.

DESIGNED AND CONSTRUCTED BY FORGE, THE EMCRAFT IS LITTLE MORE THAN A SHELL-- A REINFORCED METALLIC SPHERE--

--POWERED SOLELY BY THE ELECTROMAGNETIC MANIPULATIONS OF IT'S PILOT-- LORNA DANE--

--POLARIS.

COMPRISED OF ONLY NON-TECHNOLOGICAL COMPONENTS, IT'S CREW...

DAYTRIPPER

RICTOR

SHADOWCAT

BOOMBOOM

SIRYN

...BELIEVES THAT THE PHALANX WILL BE UNABLE TO ACCESS OR THE TINY SHIP...

ANYTHING YET?

...IT IS KURT WAGNER'S HOPE THAT THEY WILL BE UNABLE TO INFECT IT AS WELL.

WELL, ACCORDING TO THE SONAR WAVES THAT SIRYN IS PUTTING OUT--

--WE'VE SCOPED NADA IN THE WAY OF PHALANX.
AS A MATTER OF FACT--
--THERE'S NOTHING OUT THERE...

...NOTHING AT ALL.

ER...
...UM...
...HEY--
--KIT-KAT--
--I MEAN, ARE YOU GONNA BE...OKAY?
TABITHA-- THE WAY MY LIFE HAS BEEN GOING LATELY-- I DON'T KNOW IF I'M EVER GONNA BE "OKAY" AGAIN.
AFTER LOSING ILLYANA-- LOSING RACHEL--
--MY FATHER HAS MYSTERIOUSLY DISAPPEARED--
--AND NOW DOUG HAS MIRACULOUSLY RETURNED FROM THE DEAD--AND IS MERRILY LEADING US STRAIGHT INTO THE-END-OF-THE-WORLD-AS-WE-KNOW-IT...
I DON'T KNOW--
--"OKAY" SEEMS SO FAR AWAY.
HEY, IT'S ALL RELATIVE,... Y'KNOW?
LIKE SOMETIMES THINGS GET REALLY CRAZED AND YOU JUST CAN'T TAKE IT ANYMORE--
--AND THEN, JUST WHEN YOU THINK IT CAN'T GET ANY WORSE, IT DOES.
SO THEN YOU THINK--"Y'KNOW THAT FIRST PART WASN'T REALLY THAT BAD..."
BOOMER--IS THERE A POINT HERE?
WELL,... "OKAY" IS WHAT YOU MAKE IT.
BY THE EBON RINGS...!!

PAYDIRT, BOSS! WE'VE HIT THE MOTHERLODE!
THIS PLACE IS LITERALLY CRAWLING WITH PHALANX!
MEIN GOTT! HOW CAN THIS BE?
THE RADAR REGISTERS SUCH A DENSE GROUPING OF THEM--
--AND YET WHY DO WE NOT HAVE A VISUAL ON THEM--

"--WHY CAN'T WE SEE THEM...?!?"

ALL RIGHT--
--LORNA-- TAKE US DOWN-- NOW!
EVERY THING THE PHALANX DOES IS CONTINGENT ON LOGIC--THEY DON'T MAKE A MOVE UNLESS IT'S BASED ON SOME GOOD SOLID REASONING--
--AND PROBABLY CHECKED AND DOUBLE-CHECKED AT THE PHALANX "HEAD OFFICE"--THEIR COLLECTIVE INTELLIGENCE.
ANY ACTION ON THEIR PART IS LOGICAL AND RATIONAL--

--AND THEY EXPECT THE SAME FROM US!
THE ONLY WAY THEN TO DEFEAT THE PHALANX IS TO DO THE UN-EXPECTED--THE ILLOGICAL--

--AND JUST KEEP THEM GUESSING.

SO IN THE WORDS OF MY GOOD FRIEND, BOOMER--
LORNA...

"--LET'S BLOW THIS POPSICLE STAND!!!"
CHA KWOOM
LET'S TAKE IT TO THEM GANG!!

EEEEEEEEEEEEEEEEEE
HIT THEM HARD, AND FAST, AND KEEP THEM OFF-BALANCE!

NOT FAR OFF--
CHOOM CHOOM
WHAT?
NO!!!
THEY ARE ATTACKING THE BLESSED **TOWER**-- ATTEMPTING TO **TEAR DOWN THE SPIRE!!!**
I MUST GO AND STOP THEM **NOW!**
I WILL SEE THESE WALKING BLOOD SACKS ALL **DEAD** BEFORE I SEE OUR BEACON DESTROYED!
AND YET, WE STAND AMONGST MY BACK-UP PLAN, FOR SHOULD THE TOWER FALL THESE PODS SHALL YIELD FORTH A VERITABLE **LEGION** OF PHALANX WARRIORS--
--EACH ONE CONSUMED WITH CONTINUING MY PEOPLE'S **LEGACY!**
AND HOW DO YOU FARE WITH YOUR DUTIES, MAKER?
HIS HANDS AND MIND WORK FEVERISHLY, GAUGING AND STABILIZING THE POWER TO THE PODS--
--ALL THE WHILE WAGING A DESPERATE BATTLE FOR CONTROL WITHIN...
BLAST YOU, SHINAR-- YOU'RE **MANIPULATING** ME--
--**FORCING** ME TO HELP YOU AND THE PARASITES YOU WANT TO SPREAD!

IT HAS BEGUN--
--THE BEACON HAS BEEN ACTIVATED!
THE PHALANX ARE POWERING IT UP--PREPARING TO TRANSMIT THEIR DESPERATE MESSAGE ACROSS THE COSMOS.
NO. THERE IS STILL TIME FOR US TO REPROGRAM THE BEACON -- TO SCRAMBLE THE MESSAGE--
--AND REDIRECT THE TRANSMISSION AWAY FROM IT'S INTENDED COURSE!
SHOOM
SHUK CHING
DOUG--IS THERE NOTHING WE CAN DO FOR THE POOR VILLAGERS...?
...ANY WAY T'REVERSE WHAT THE PHALANX HAVE DONE T' THEM?
WE'RE TOO LATE, THEN...
...WE GOT HERE TOO LATE?
THESE HUMANS WERE CO-OPTED BY THE PHALANX, RAHNE-- THEIR LIFE-FORCES ARE BEING USED AS A CONDUIT FOR THE ENERGY THAT POWERS THE BEACON.
IF THAT POWER WERE BLOCKED, THOSE LIFE ENERGIES WOULD BE "BACKED-UP" -- PUSHED BACK INTO THE VILLAGERS' BODIES.
TO "JAM" THE ENERGY FLOW, HOWEVER, WOULD NECESSITATE THE SACRIFICE OF A SINGLE LIFE FORCE--
I'LL DO THAT.
SEEING AS THIS WHOLE MESS IS PRETTY MUCH MY FAULT...

AT THE BASE OF THE SPIRE--
REMEMBER, EVERYBODY--
--THAT TOWER IS MADE OF PEOPLE-- INNOCENT VILLAGERS WHO HAVE BEEN MESMERIZED BY THE PHALANX--
--SO BE CAREFUL!!!
FIGHT HARD--BUT BE CAREFUL!
WE CAN'T RISK KILLING ANY OF THOSE PEOPLE!!
NO!! YOU CANNOT!!!
CRRAKK!
SHRUK

HUMANITY IS DOOMED!! --001011--
FIP FIP
BOOM BOOM
THE PHALANX IS EVERYWHERE-- AND ONCE THE BEACON IS ACTIVATED, YOUR VILE RACE WILL BE BUT A MEMORY IN THE--10011 --HISTORY OF THIS PLANET!
ONCE OUR FORE-BEARERS EMERGE --WE WILL BURY YOU!!
YOU MAY HAVE WON THIS BATTLE HERE, BUT EVEN NOW YOUR OWN FORGE LABORS TO ASSURE OUR SUCCESS!!

MEANWHILE... AT THE TOP OF THE BEACON...
SAM--YE MUS' BE DAFT!!
HOW COULD YE POSSIBLY BELIEVE THAT YE'D BE RESPONSIBLE F'R ANY O' THIS?!?
'CAUSE DOUG DIED ON MY WATCH...
...AH WAS LEADIN' TH' NEW MUTANTS WHEN HE WAS...
...WHEN YOU WERE...
...THAT MAKES ME RESPONSIBLE F'R EVERYTHING THAT HAPPENED AFTERWARDS.
SAM--WHILE I AM NOT DOUG RAMSEY--AS MUCH AS EVERY-ONE, IT SEEMS, WOULD LIKE ME TO BE--
--I DO HAVE A LIMITED ACCESS TO HIS MEMORIES. I KNOW HOW HE FELT ABOUT YOU... I KNOW HE WOULD NEVER BLAME YOU FOR HIS DEATH.
JUST AS I KNOW HE WOULD NEVER ASK YOU TO DO SOMETHING THAT IS HIS PLACE TO DO...
WHA--? DOUG--NO!!!
CHOOOSH!
NO, DOUG. NO.
WE CANNAE LOSE YE AGAIN...

THE POD GARDEN.
FORGE!
BAMF
SIRYN SAID THERE WAS AN OUTLYING CLUSTER OF READ--
VAS IST...?
FORGE--WHAT IN THE NAME OF GOD ARE YOU DOING?!
THEY'RE MAKING ME HELP THEM--DRAWING OUT EVERY IMPULSE OF MY MUTANT ABILITIES?!
WELL, FIGHT IT!!
YOU'RE NOT JUST A MUTANT, MEIN FREUND-- YOU ARE A HUMAN AS WELL! DRAW ON THAT--
--ON THE STRENGTH OF YOUR CONVICTIONS AS A HUMAN-- DRAW ON THE PART OF YOU THAT IS THE MOST HUMAN.
DRAW ON YOUR HUMAN SPIRIT.

FORGE-- IF THESE PHALANX EMERGE--
--IF THEY GET THE CHANCE TO BE RE-LEASED ONTO MANKIND--
--THERE'LL BE NO MORE LIFE AS WE KNOW IT--NO MORE MUSIC OR ART--NO MORE MAGIC--
--NO MORE US!!
LOOK-- THEY'RE GLOWING-- THEY'LL BE OPEN-ING ANY MINUTE-- YOU HAVE TO STOP THEM NOW!
I UNDERSTAND, KURT-- BUT THEY'RE FORCING ME TO KEEP CREATING-- WAIT-- MAYBE IF I CAN HARNESS MY MUTANT POWER FOR JUST A SECOND--
--I CAN FORCE MYSELF TO CREATE SOMETHING THAT WILL BLOCK THE POWER TO THE PODS!
hurrr--
aaAAAAAAARRGH!
FIGHT IT, MEIN FREUND, FIGHT IT!!
THEIR INFLUENCE --ungh!-- IS SO STRONG--
--TOO STRONG...
I DON'T KNOW, KURT...
I DON'T KNOW IF I CAN DO IT...

CHOOOOOOM
OH, DOUG--
SAM-- DO YE THINK--
POOM
HE'S GONE, RAHNE--
--AH --AH DON'T THINK HE MADE IT...
POOM
THE RESULTS OF DOUGLOCK'S ACTIONS ARE SPECTACULAR--
POOM
--AS THE TRANSMISSION OF THE BEACON IS "JAMMED"-- THE LIFE-ENERGIES ARE RETURNED TO THE HUMAN HOSTS FROM WHICH THEY WERE STOLEN!!
POOOM
WITH THE "LIVING CIRCUIT" WHICH WAS THE BEACON NOW BROKEN--UNCHECKED ENERGIES BOMBARD THE TECHNO-ORGANIC BINDINGS OF THE TOWER--
--OVERLOADING THE PHALANX WITH POWER IT COULD NEVER DARE TO HARNESS!!
THE EXPLOSION CAN BE SEEN AND HEARD THROUGHOUT THE VALLEY, AND AS THE BABEL SPIRE FALLS, THERE IS A SOUND THAT RISES UP AND ABOVE THE CACOPHONOUS DIN OF DESTRUCTION--
--IT IS THE SOUND OF THE PHALANX SCREAMING!!

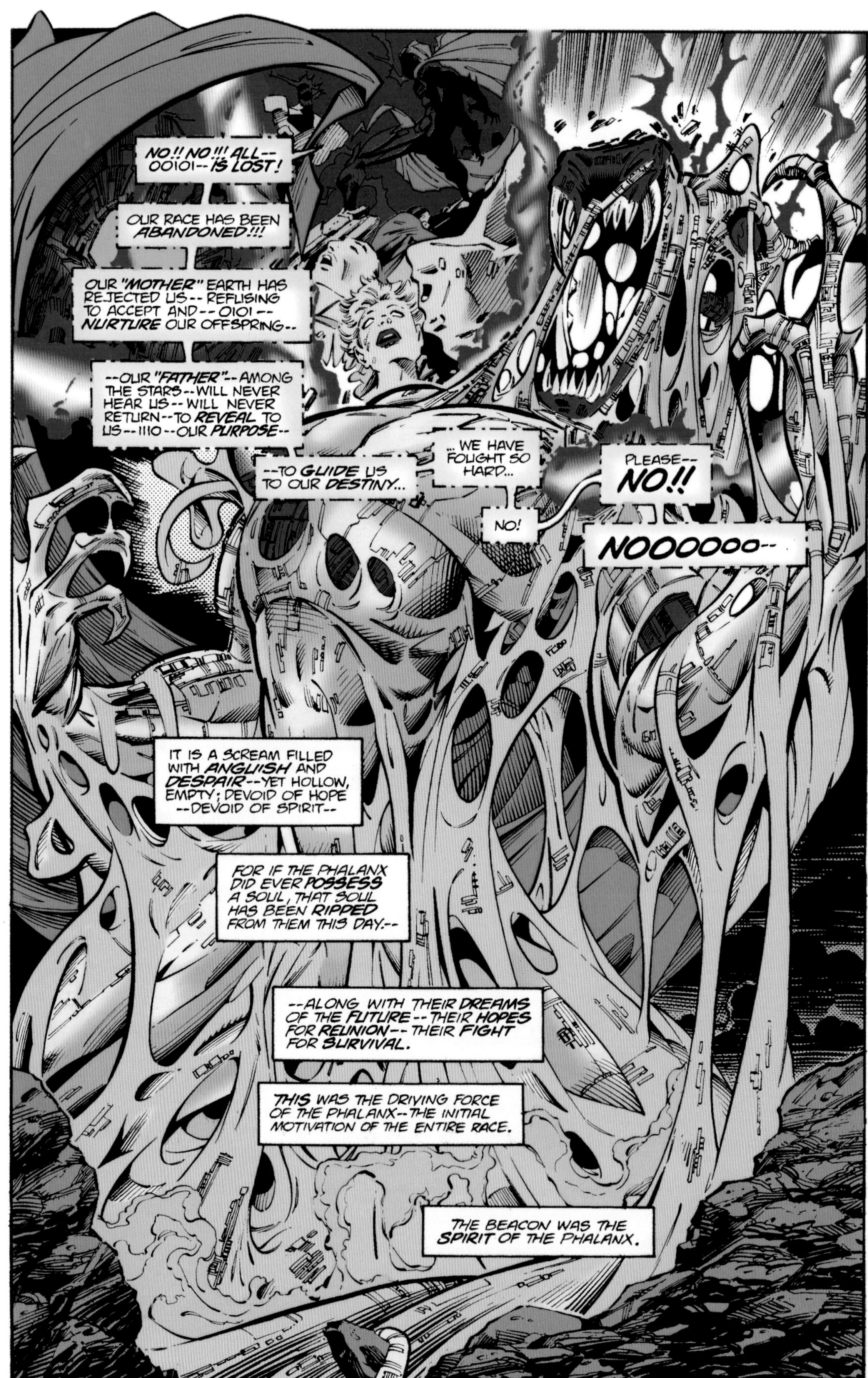
NO!! NO!!! ALL-- 00101-- IS LOST!
OUR RACE HAS BEEN ABANDONED!!!
OUR "MOTHER" EARTH HAS REJECTED US-- REFUSING TO ACCEPT AND-- 0101-- NURTURE OUR OFFSPRING--
--OUR "FATHER"-- AMONG THE STARS-- WILL NEVER HEAR US-- WILL NEVER RETURN-- TO REVEAL TO US-- 1110-- OUR PURPOSE--
--TO GUIDE US TO OUR DESTINY...
...WE HAVE FOUGHT SO HARD...
NO!
PLEASE-- NO!!
NOOOOOO--
IT IS A SCREAM FILLED WITH ANGUISH AND DESPAIR-- YET HOLLOW, EMPTY; DEVOID OF HOPE --DEVOID OF SPIRIT--
FOR IF THE PHALANX DID EVER POSSESS A SOUL, THAT SOUL HAS BEEN RIPPED FROM THEM THIS DAY.--
--ALONG WITH THEIR DREAMS OF THE FUTURE-- THEIR HOPES FOR REUNION-- THEIR FIGHT FOR SURVIVAL.
THIS WAS THE DRIVING FORCE OF THE PHALANX-- THE INITIAL MOTIVATION OF THE ENTIRE RACE.
THE BEACON WAS THE SPIRIT OF THE PHALANX.

--AS IT FALLS, SO DO THE PHALANX, REAL-IZING THAT IT IS OVER-- THE BATTLE IS LOST--
--THERE IS NOTHING LEFT TO FIGHT FOR.

LOOKIT ALL THAT GLOP! WHATEVER IT WAS DOUG DID--IT SURE TOOK THE PHALANX OUTTA TH' PICTURE IN A BIG WAY!
HE REALLY SAVED OUR HIDES.

YOU WERE RIGHT ABOUT HIM, RAHNE. THERE WAS A LOT MORE O' TH' REAL DOUG IN THERE THAN AH WAS WILLIN' T'BELIEVE...
AH'M SORRY AH WOULDN'T BELIEVE YOU--
--AH JUST COULDN'T SEE 'IM WITH YOUR EYES...
DINNAE APOLOGIZE F'R YUIR FEELIN'S SAM... YE'RE ONLY BE'IN HONEST...
I JUST WISH...

DOUG DESTROYED THE BEACON, HE FREED THOSE POOR PEOPLE... HE TURNED THOSE HORRIBLE PHALANX INTO OOZE--
--BUT HE WAS PART OF THE PHALANX HIMSELF--AN' WE HAD ONLY JUST GOTTEN HIM BACK AGAIN--
--AN' NOW HE'S GONE--
--AN' WE NEVER GOT TH' CHANCE T'TELL 'IM--

--OR MY HUMANITY I WAS FIGHTING FOR...!
THE END

TONY DANIEL
KEVIN KONRAD
MASON

MARVEL COMICS
X-FORCE
© 1994 MARVEL ENT. GROUP, INC.
$1.50 US
$2.05 CAN/UK £1.25
39
OCT
01766
APPROVED BY THE COMICS CODE AUTHORITY
TONY DANIEL
KEVIN CONRAD

EVEN LATE INTO THE NIGHT, THE WINDS SWEEP HOT ACROSS THE ARIZONA DESERT SANDS OF THE ABANDONED CAMP VERDE APACHE RESERVATION.
HIDDEN FROM VIEW BENEATH THOSE SANDS AND RUINS, LIES THE BUNKER HEADQUARTERS OF THE OUTLAW MUTANT REBELS KNOWN AS X-FORCE.
AND CAUTIOUSLY MAKING HER WAY THROUGH THOSE TUNNELS IS DOMINO, THE TEAM'S MYSTERIOUS "MOTHER-FIGURE"...
CABLE
SIRYN
WARPATH
BOOMER
CANNONBALL
DOMINO
RICTOR
SHATTERSTAR
...MOTHER TERESA BY WAY OF RIPLEY FROM THE MOVIE, "ALIENS."
A WOMAN WHO, LOOKING AT HER SENSOR-PAD, HAS COME TO A TENSE REALI-ZATION...
WHATEVER WAS HERE...
...HAS GONE TOPSIDE.
AND GUESS WHO'S GOING TO BE DUMB ENOUGH TO CHASE AFTER IT?
ANOTHER HARD-HITTING
X-FORCE GANG-GAB LOVE-FEST!

HAVING SPENT THE LAST WEEK SCOUTING POTENTIAL NEW HEADQUARTER SITES FOR THE TEAM--
--DOMINO RETURNED AN HOUR AGO, ONLY TO FIND THE BUNKER ABANDONED AND COMPLETELY DRAINED OF POWER.
ALL THE INTERNAL SYSTEMS WERE OFF-LINE.
STAN LEE PRESENTS
LETTING GO
...FOR IT APPEARS, AS RICTOR WOULD PUT IT--
--THAT I AM SERIOUSLY "SPAZZING OUT"--!

ELECTRICAL FIRE FLASHES CHARRED THE WALLS THROUGHOUT THE NETWORK OF UNDERGROUND CORRIDORS.
SOMETHING HAD COME AND-- JUST AS QUICKLY-- GONE.
BUT WHO-- OR WHAT-- WAS IT?
DOMINO, MY DEAR...
...I COULD USE SOME ASSISTANCE...
!?!
A STORY OF FRIENDSHIP AND SACRIFICE BROUGHT TO YOU BY
FABIAN NICIEZA · TONY DANIEL · KEVIN CONRAD
WRITER PENCILER INKER
CHRIS ELIOPOULOS LETTERER
MARIE JAVINS COLORIST
BOB HARRAS HANGING ON
TOM DEFALCO STANDING BY

-MMMFF-
ODD, I ANTICIPATED, FROM THE ANGLE OF MY DESCENT--
--THAT I WOULD HAVE LANDED DIRECTLY ON TOP OF YOU, CAUSING SUBSTANTIAL INJURIES.

YEAH, WELL, THINGS TEND TO GO MY WAY, YOU KNOW?
NOW, DO YOU MIND EXPLAINING WHO YOU ARE BEFORE I DO SOME PLASMA TRACER DENTAL WORK ON YOU--
--ASSUMING YOU HAVE TEETH, THAT IS.
WHY, BEATRICE, I HAVE KNOWN THE PLEASURE OF YOUR COMPANY FOR YEARS--

--ALTHOUGH, YOU DID NOT OFFICIALLY MAKE MY ACQUAINTANCE UNTIL QUITE RECENTLY.
AN' IF THE FACE AIN'T FAMILIAR, TOOTS--
--I WOULD HOPE THE VOICE IS!

PROFESSOR--?!
THE SENTIENT OPERATIONAL PROGRAM THAT RUNS CABLE'S CYBERNET SYSTEMS?!
BUT THAT'S NOT POSSIBLE!

INDEED IT IS, MY FRIEND. ALTHOUGH, IF YOU DON'T MIND--
--I WOULD PREFER TO BE CALLED PROSH.
IT IS AN AMALGAM OF WHAT I ONCE WAS, WHAT I AM NOW--
--AND PERHAPS, WITH THE HELP OF ALL MY FRIENDS--
--WHAT I MAY YET ONE DAY BE!
BEFORE WE DO THAT THOUGH, IT WOULD APPEAR I MAY REQUIRE SOME PHYSICAL ASSISTANCE RETURNING TO THE BUNKER--
--FOR IT SEEMS, I HAVE FINALLY DRAINED MY STORAGE CELLS COMPLETELY DRY...
...OF...MY...REMAINING--POWER--
CHIKKZZ
SHIKTT SHIKTT
HMM--?
OH, MY, IS THIS WHAT WAKING UP FEELS LIKE?
HOW EXHAUSTING AND EX-HILARATING--BOTH AT ONCE!
THERE! I DO MOST CERTAINLY FEEL RATHER REFRESHED NOW.
GOOD.
NOW MAYBE YOU CAN MAKE THE REST OF US FEEL BETTER...

... IF YOU'D TELL US WHAT THE FLONQ IS GOING ON?!
NATHAN? AND THE REST OF X-FORCE, AS WELL!
HOW WONDERFUL TO SEE YOU ALL.
I TAKE IT THEN, THAT THINGS WENT RATHER WELL AGAINST THE PHALANX*? GOOD, GOOD.
MY OWN UNEXPECTED ENCOUNTER WITH ONE OF THEM HERE AT THE BUNKER COMPLEX--
--AS YOU CAN SEE--HAS LEFT ME IN A RATHER... INTERESTING... POSITION.
*LAST ISSUE. --BOB
BY THE WAY, HOW LONG HAVE I BEEN INACTIVE?

ABOUT SEVENTY-EIGHT HOURS NOW, PROF.
PROSH, IF YOU PLEASE, JAMES. WITH AN "S-H". SAY IT WITH ME...
SH-OOR. PROSH. I LIKE THE SOUND OF THAT.
DOMINO DRAGGED YOU BACK HERE AN' PLUGGED YOU INTO THE SECONDARY FUSION GENERATORS--
--AN' YOU'VE BEEN FEEDIN' OFF THE BUNKER'S POWER SUPPLY EVER SINCE.
KINDA SKINNY FOR SUCH A HUNGRY DUDE, EH, AMIGO?
CLINK CLINK
WHY, JULIO, I CAN ONLY GET AS BIG AND STRONG AS YOU ARE--
--IF I AM ALLOWED TO EAT LIKE A GROWING BOY SHOULD!
'ZACTLY HOW DID YOU GET THE HUNKY BOD, PROSH?
TABITHA, THE EXACT DETAILS ARE A BIT CONFUSING TO ME--
SNAP
--BUT I CAN ACTIVATE THE BUNKER'S SECURITY CAMERAS--
--TO PLAY BACK THE PHALANX ATTACK WHICH LED TO MY CURRENT CONDITION.

"AN AGENT OF THE PHALANX CAME TO CAMP VERDE --
"--LOOKING TO ASSIMILATE ALL OF YOU, I IMAGINE--
"--BUT WHEN HE TRIED TO INFILTRATE MY CYBERNET--
"--THE POOR FELLOW WAS IN FOR A RATHER SHOCKING SURPRISE.
I GUESS I FOUND THAT MOST ENJOYABLE OF ALL--
--BECAUSE I RAN TOO LONG AND TOO FAR--
--LOSING POWER, AND NEARLY MY NEWFOUND LIFE AS WELL, UNTIL BEATRICE FOUND ME.
"HIS FORM WAS COMPLETELY DISCORPORATED--
"--LOST TO THE OVERWHELMING FLOW OF INFORMATION AMASSED IN MY NEURAL NET.
"BUT WHAT THE PHALANX LOST, I APPARENTLY GAINED--
" --NAMELY, A CORPOREAL FORM-- A BODY--
BEATRICE?
NOT ANOTHER WORD.
"-- FOR THE FIRST TIME IN MY LONG LIFE, I COULD SEE FROM MY OWN EYES--
"-- I COULD TASTE THE AIR, SMELL THE DESERT FLOWERS--
"-- AND I COULD RUN!!"

ALL'S WELL, PROSH, 'CAUSE YOU GOT YOURSELF A GREAT SET OF GAMS FOR ALL THE HASSLES.

WAIT A MINUTE, FOLKS, JUST TO PLAY DEVIL'S ADVOCATE HERE--

--BUT AFTER WHAT WE WENT THROUGH WITH THE PHALANX--HOW DO WE KNOW THE PROSH ISN'T--

--ANOTHER KILLER ROBOT, MY DEAR DOMINO?

YOUR DOUBTS ARE LOGICAL, BUT TOTALLY UNFOUNDED. BUT HOW WOULD YOU FEEL ABOUT A "LADY-KILLER" ROBOT?

SMEK

DOM--STAND DOWN. THERE'S AS MUCH A CHANCE OF THE PROFESSOR--

--I'M SORRY! --PROSH-- BEING A THREAT TO US, AS THERE IS OF ME TRAVELLING THROUGH TIME.

AH THOUGHT YOU COULD DO THAT.

THAT WAS BEFORE GRAYMALKIN WAS LOST TO US AND THE TIME DISPLACEMENT CORE WAS TAKEN OFF-LINE, SAMUEL.

THOUGH IF ONLY NATHAN WOULD WAKE UP REGARDING THE TRUE NATURE OF HIS POWERS...

...AH, BUT THAT IS FOR ANOTHER TIME.
AND WHAT ARE YOU LOOKING AT? FOR YEARS I'VE MADE YOU COFFEE YOU TOLD ME WAS "WORTH KILLING FOR."
NOW THAT I FINALLY HAVE A MOUTH, I'D LIKE TO SEE WHAT THE FUSS WAS ALL ABOUT...

FEH. THAT WASN'T WORTH IT.
YOU DO REALIZE THIS IS NOTHING MORE THAN WATER FILTERED THROUGH CRUSHED ROASTED BEANS ?
ARE YOU MAKING FUN OF COFFEE ?
YE TEMPT DEATH, PROSH, T'BE DISPARAGING CABLE'S VERY LIFE'S BLOOD!
'STAR-- HOW COME YOU'RE NOT HANGING OUT WITH THE REST OF US ?

I DO NOT WISH TO RAIN ON ANYONE'S CHARADE, WARPATH--
--BUT I HAVE BEEN MONITORING PROSH'S ENERGY INTAKE.

BY ALL MEANS, SHATTERSTAR, RAIN ON OUR "CHARADE"-- WHAT'VE YOU FOUND ?
ACTUALLY, NOTHING. AND THAT'S WHAT'S SO STRANGE ABOUT ALL THIS--
--THE EQUIPMENT SHOULD BE REGISTERING THE OUTPUT DRAINAGE, BUT I'M GETTING A FLATLINE READING.
PERHAPS PROSH'S PRESENCE IS SOMEHOW INTERFERING WITH THE THE DIASNOSTIC EQUIPMENT ?
NO! THAT CAN'T BE!
YOU MUST BE READING IT WRONG!
WHEN DID YOU BECOME A SPECIALIST IN FUSION ENERGY DRAINAGE SYSTEMS?
NATHAN, DON'T SPEAK ON SUBJECTS YOU KNOW NOTHING ABOUT.
FIVE HOURS AFTER I FIRST TAUGHT SHATTER-STAR TO PLAY CHESS--
--I NEVER WON ANOTHER GAME AGAINST THE LAD, SO DON'T BELITTLE HIS INTELLI-GENCE.

NAH, WE'LL JUST BELITTLE HIS LACK OF PERSONALITY.
I'M KIDDING, 'STAR-- PUT THAT SWORD DOWN!
SERIOUSLY, GANG, SHOULD WE BE CONCERNED ABOUT THE QUANTITY OF ENERGY IT MAY TAKE TO KEEP PROSH MOBILE?
I PROMISE I WON'T DEPLETE TOO MUCH OF YOUR RESERVES, JAMES.
I'LL BE A GOOD BOY AND YOU'LL STILL HAVE ENOUGH POWER TO GO FIGHT THOSE NASTY, BAD MUTANTS!
I THINK JAMES WAS WORRIED A LITTLE BIT MORE ABOUT THE REFRIGERATOR!
HMMM. WELL, HE'S SHEER OUT OF LUCK THEN, THERESA. YOU CAN STARVE FOR ALL I CARE!
I CAN SEE THIS HAS DE-GENERATED PRETTY QUICKLY.
NO SENSE TRYING TO FIGURE OUT ANY SOLUTIONS RIGHT NOW, I GUESS.

THERE AIN'T REALLY THAT MUCH OF A PROBLEM, JIMMY.
PROSH IS ALIVE, THAT'S WHAT MATTERS. IF IT MEANS WE GOTTA CONSERVE OUR STUPID ENERGY SUP-PLY, SO WHAT?
EVEN IF IT MEANS YOU CAIN'T USE YOUR BLOW-DRYER NO MORE, BOOMER?
OH. LET THE TRANSFORMER ROT, I SAY!

APPARENTLY, PROSH, THIS LITTLE... CHANGE... IN YOU HAS BROUGHT OUT QUITE A BIT OF LIFE IN THE REST OF US.
I THINK I'M SPEAKING FOR EVERY-ONE HERE WHEN I SAY--IT'S A PLEASURE TO WELCOME YOU TO X-FORCE!
NATHAN, THOUGH I HAVE ALWAYS CONSIDERED MYSELF A PART OF YOU, AND YOUR ENTIRE FAMILY HERE--
--ALLOW ME TO SAY, FOR THE RECORD, THAT THE PLEASURE IS ALL MINE!

DAYS PASS. AND, FOR A CHANGE OF PACE, IT IS A RELAXING TIME.
PROSH QUICKLY BECOMES BOTH A TEACHER OF AND PUPIL TO THE YOUNG MUTANTS AT THE BUNKER COMPLEX.
HIS WARMTH AND COMPASSION SERVE AS A PERFECT FOCAL POINT TO THE NEEDS HE SHARES IN COMMON WITH THESE YOUNG PEOPLE.
THE NEED FOR DIRECTION, FOR HOPE, FOR A SENSE OF BEING AND BELONGING.

AND MOST OF ALL, THE NEED...
ACH! SUN IN MY EYES! GIVE ME A COLD BREEZE WHISTLIN' OFF CLEW BAY ANYDAY.
WHAT IS THAT THEY'RE DOING--?

...TO HAVE SOME FUN!!
...ULP!

OH NO...

TACKLED!
OOOOMPH
SACKED FOR A TWENTY YARD LOSS!
AND SO, HAVING RECRUITED THE YOUNG APACHE FROM OUT OF NO-WHERE--

--BUDDY RYAN HAS TURNED ARIZONA CARDINALS INTO A CONTENDER!
WILL TERESA BE JOINING US?
MAYBE IF'N YE CHOOSE T'PLAY REAL FOOTBALL.

FEKT, SOCCER LACKS THE PHYSICAL STIMULATION OF AMERICAN FOOTBALL!
SKINS' BALL!
SHIRTS AND SKINS? WHICH SIDE IS PROSH ON?
HE INSISTED ON PLAYING FOR SKINS. GO FIGURE.
HE SAID, "IF I'M GOING TO HAVE ONE, I'LL FLAUNT IT EVERY CHANCE I GET!"
SPEAKING OF ANY CHANCE I GET...
I KNOW.
BUT I'D RATHER NOT.
JIMMY... DON'T--
--I--
UHM... JIMMY... YE CAN PUT ME DOWN NOW, Y'KNOW.
THONK
AYA! ARE WE PLAYIN' BALL HERE, OR WHAT? VAMANOS, EH?

YOU DON'T HAVE TO KEEP AVOIDING THEM JUST BECAUSE OF ME, DOM.
I KNOW, NATE. BUT THEY WERE LIED TO ENOUGH BY SOME-ONE WEARING MY FACE, WHEN VANESSA IM-PERSONATED ME--
--THAT I'D RATHER NOT GIVE THEM ANY REASONS TO MISTRUST ME.
I DON'T WANT YOU TO LIE FOR ME--BUT I DON'T WANT THEM TO KNOW YET, EITHER.
I WANT THEM ALL--ESPECIALLY PROSH--TO ENJOY THE FUN THEY'VE BEEN HAVING.
EVEN IF IT KILLS YOU, NATE?
WELL, AT LEAST UNTIL WE FIND SOME HARD EVIDENCE THAT PROSH'S NEW LIFE REALLY DOES HAVE SOMETHING TO DO--
--WITH WHAT'S HAPPENED TO ME!
IT'S TOO SIMILAR TO THE CHANGE YOU WENT THROUGH WHEN YOUR ARM INTERACTED WITH NIMROD'S NEURAL NET-WORK LAST MONTH.
THE CONTINUAL CONTROL YOUR MIND NEEDS TO EXERT ON THE TECHNO-ORGANIC PORTION OF YOUR BODY IS BEING DISRUPTED BY SOMETHING--
--AND IF IT KEEPS UP, NATHAN--IT'S GOING TO TEAR YOU APART!

THAT EVENING...
YO, SHATTY-- WHY'D YOU SKIP OUT ON DINNER?
IT WAS MY TURN TO COOK TONIGHT, TOO. TOTAL DISASTER AREA! THE TEMP GAUGE ON THE OVEN WAS SHOT AND I DIDN'T KNOW IT.
SHOULDA SEEN GUTHRIE'S FACE WHEN HE BIT INTO THE CHICKEN...
I IMAGINE IT WAS QUITE COMICAL.
WHAT'RE YOU UP TO IN HERE? YOU SET UP A VCR PLAYBACK FOR A "LOVE CONNECTION" MARATHON AGAIN?
THE REMOTE SELECTOR IS NOT OPERATING PROPERLY. I HAVE BEEN TRYING TO FIX IT FOR OVER AN HOUR.
D'YOU CHECK THE BATTERIES, DUDE?
HUMPH.
WHAT I HAVE DONE IS PERFORM A COMPLETE DIAGNOSTIC ON ALL OUR COMMUNICATIONS SYSTEMS.
AND I HAVE NOT LIKED WHAT I HAVE UNCOVERED.
ACCORDING TO THIS, SOMETHING'S PITCHIN' A FREQUENCY BROADCAST WHICH IS SCRAMBLING ALL OUR ELECTROMAGNETIC LINKS.
INDEED. A PERPETUAL HAZE OF STATIC INCURSION INTO EVERYTHING HERE WHICH RUNS ON ANY KIND OF ENERGY SOURCE.
AND I AM AFRAID, I HAVE ALSO GONE A LONG WAY TOWARDS IDENTIFYING THE SOURCE...
...AND IT CONFIRMS MY INITIAL SUSPICIONS FROM DAYS AGO!

MORNING...
...INSIDE THE HANGAR BAY...
WELL, THIS IS GONNA BE A HECKUVA LOT MORE WORK THAN I THOUGHT.
"JUST GONNA GO REROUTE THE FUSION PLASMA INVERTERS--Y'ALL WANNA HELP OUT OR WHAT, JIMMY? HA-YUCK, HA-YUCK!"
I NEVER SAID "Y'ALL" AND AH ONLY USED ONE "HA-YUCK."
AH GUESS WE BETTER FIND CABLE AN' TELL HIM THE IPAC IS GROWIN' BIG METAL ZITS ALL OVER IT.
IF YOU CAN FIND HIM. NO ONE'S SEEN HIM SINCE YESTERDAY MORNING.
DOMINO ONLY SAID HE WAS HAVING A REALLY BAD HAIR DAY.
AN' AH HATE T'THINK WHAT BOOMER SAID IN RESPONSE.
HMM. SO WHAT NOW?
WE GOTTA FIND OUT WHAT--OR WHO--
"--IS RESPONSIBLE FOR THIS."
ME--?!

YES, PROSH, IT IS YOU--
--S'MUCH-- ASSS I DIDN' WAN' IT TO BE TRUE-- HAFF
--THE ENERGY SIGNATURES YOU EXIST ON --THE TRANSMISSIONS RUNNIN' THROUGH YOU... LIKE BLOOD THROUGH US--
--YOUR MECHANICAL EQUIVALENT TO OUR DNA--ISSS DISRUPTIN' EV'RYTHIN' IN THE BUNKER--
--INCLUDIN'... MY T-O MESH!
IF MY VERY EXISTENCE HAS BEEN DOING THIS TO YOU--
--THEN THE SOLUTION IS LOGICAL. I MUST CEASE TO EXIST.
NO! YOU JUST FOUND LIFE--REAL LIFE--F'R THE FIRST TIME--
--I WON' BE THE REASON FOR TAKIN' IT... FROM YOU!
BUT, I CANNOT LIVE WHILE YOU SUFFER.
WHAT ELSE CAN BE DONE TO STOP THIS?
WE--WE DON'T KNOW, PROSH.
BUT I THINK IT'S TIME WE GOT EVERY-ONE IN ON THIS.

"AND MAYBE TOGETHER, WE'LL BE ABLE TO FIGURE SOMETHING OUT!"
MADRE DE DIOS--CABLE'S A MESS! WE CAN'T EVEN GET A DECENT READING OUT OF THE MEDICAL SCANNERS!
THIS IS ALL BECAUSE OF ME!
I HAVE CORRUPTED EVERYTHING ALL OF YOU HAVE TRIED TO BUILD HERE!
I HAVE TO DISCORPORATE--TRY AND PURGE THIS FROM WITHIN MY NEURAL NET, WHICH IS LINKED TO ALL THE SYSTEMS HERE IN THE BUNKER.
AND ARE YOU AWARE, PROSH, THAT TO DO SO WOULD, IN ESSENCE, END YOUR PHYSICAL LIFE?
THAT WHICH YOU SEEK TO PURGE IS ALSO RESPONSIBLE FOR HAVING GIVEN YOU THIS PRESENT FORM.
I KNOW, GAVEEDRA-SEVEN. I KNOW EXACTLY WHAT I HAVE TO DO.
GAVEEDRA-HUH?
THERE HAS TO BE A BETTER SOLUTION THAN THAT.
THERE HAS TO BE A WAY FOR YOU TO LIVE AND FOR US TO LIVE, TOO.
WHAT'S KILLING ME--IS KEEPING YOU ALIVE!
SO HOW ABOUT SAVING ME AT THE SAME TIME AS YOU SAVE YOURSELF?
WHY NOT JUST TAKE EVERYTHING HERE WITH YOU AND LEAVE?

BUT NATHAN-- THAT WOULD MEAN YOU WOULD LOSE ALL OF YOUR EQUIPMENT AND MOST OF YOUR DATA-NETWORK--
THEY'RE JUST THINGS, PROSH. THEY USED TO MATTER TO ME WHEN THAT WAS ALL I HAD--
--BUT PEOPLE MATTER MORE TO ME. YOUR LIFE AND HAPPINESS MATTER MORE!
BUT IF I WERE TO LEAVE--I WOULD NEVER BE ABLE TO SEE YOU AGAIN.
BUT YOU'D BE ALIVE, PROSH. OUT THERE SOMEWHERE, IN THE STARS! THINK ABOUT HOW MUCH THERE IS FOR YOU T' DISCOVER!
IT WOULD BE... WONDERFUL... TO BE SOARING THROUGH THE COSMOS AGAIN.
MY PEOPLE'S BURIAL GROUND IS A MILE SOUTHEAST OF HERE. THAT'S THE ONLY PLACE WHICH I ASK YOU TO LEAVE UNTOUCHED.
AS FOR THE REST OF THIS PLACE...
JAMES, FOR ME TO DO THIS WOULD REQUIRE THAT I SEVERELY DISRUPT THE FOUNDATIONS OF THIS CAMP.
NOT JUST THE BUNKER COMPLEX, BUT MANY OF THE BUILDINGS ABOVE WOULD NEED TO BE CO-OPTED INTO MY MASS, AS WELL, TO PROPERLY PREPARE THIS FORM FOR INTERSTELLAR TRAVEL.

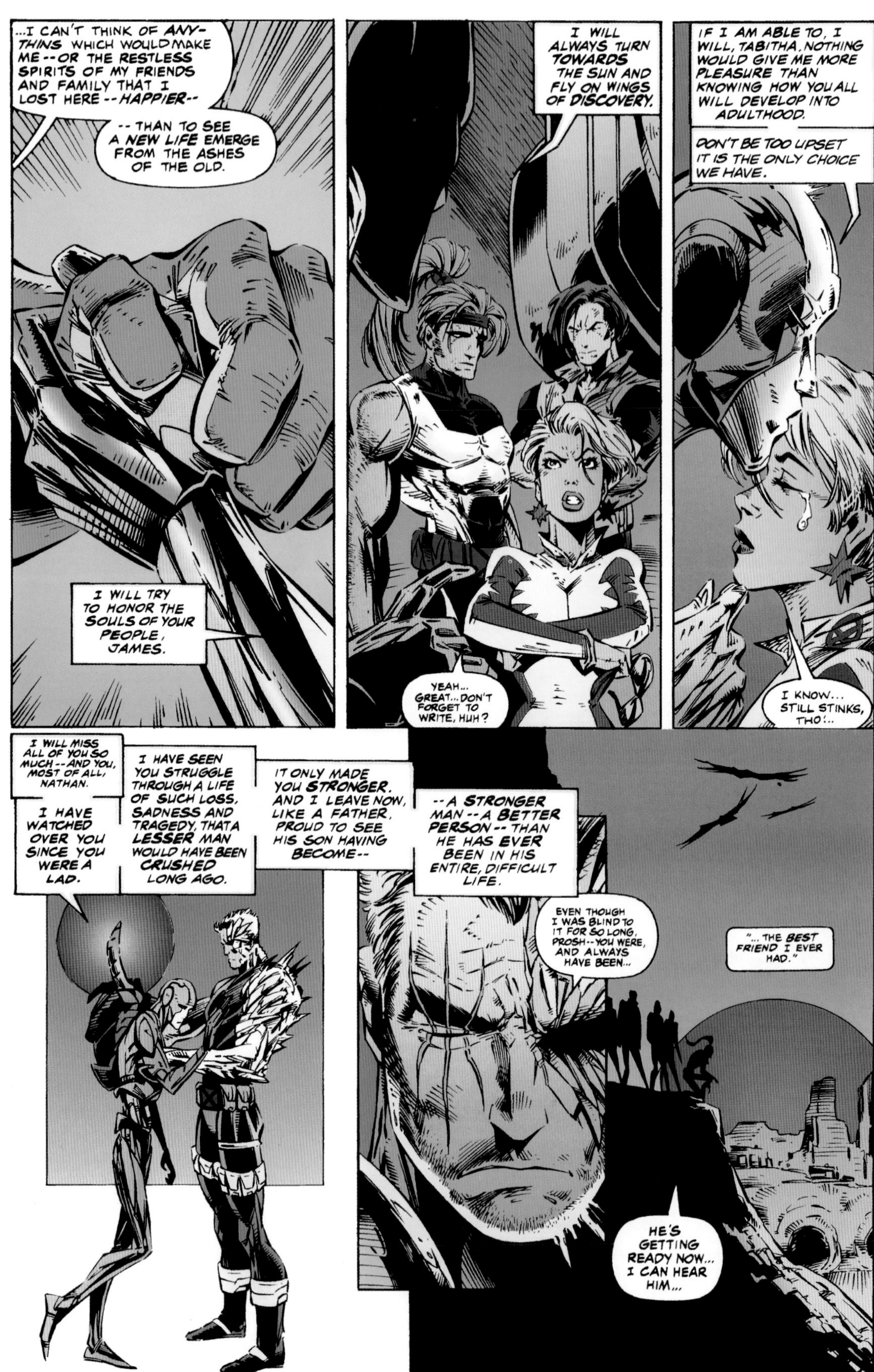
...I CAN'T THINK OF ANYTHING WHICH WOULD MAKE ME -- OR THE RESTLESS SPIRITS OF MY FRIENDS AND FAMILY THAT I LOST HERE -- HAPPIER--
-- THAN TO SEE A NEW LIFE EMERGE FROM THE ASHES OF THE OLD.
I WILL TRY TO HONOR THE SOULS OF YOUR PEOPLE, JAMES.
I WILL ALWAYS TURN TOWARDS THE SUN AND FLY ON WINGS OF DISCOVERY.
YEAH... GREAT... DON'T FORGET TO WRITE, HUH?
IF I AM ABLE TO, I WILL, TABITHA. NOTHING WOULD GIVE ME MORE PLEASURE THAN KNOWING HOW YOU ALL WILL DEVELOP INTO ADULTHOOD.
DON'T BE TOO UPSET IT IS THE ONLY CHOICE WE HAVE.
I KNOW... STILL STINKS, THO'...
I WILL MISS ALL OF YOU SO MUCH -- AND YOU, MOST OF ALL, NATHAN.
I HAVE WATCHED OVER YOU SINCE YOU WERE A LAD.
I HAVE SEEN YOU STRUGGLE THROUGH A LIFE OF SUCH LOSS, SADNESS AND TRAGEDY, THAT A LESSER MAN WOULD HAVE BEEN CRUSHED LONG AGO.
IT ONLY MADE YOU STRONGER. AND I LEAVE NOW, LIKE A FATHER, PROUD TO SEE HIS SON HAVING BECOME--
-- A STRONGER MAN -- A BETTER PERSON -- THAN HE HAS EVER BEEN IN HIS ENTIRE, DIFFICULT LIFE.
EVEN THOUGH I WAS BLIND TO IT FOR SO LONG, PROSH -- YOU WERE, AND ALWAYS HAVE BEEN...
"... THE BEST FRIEND I EVER HAD."
HE'S GETTING READY NOW... I CAN HEAR HIM...

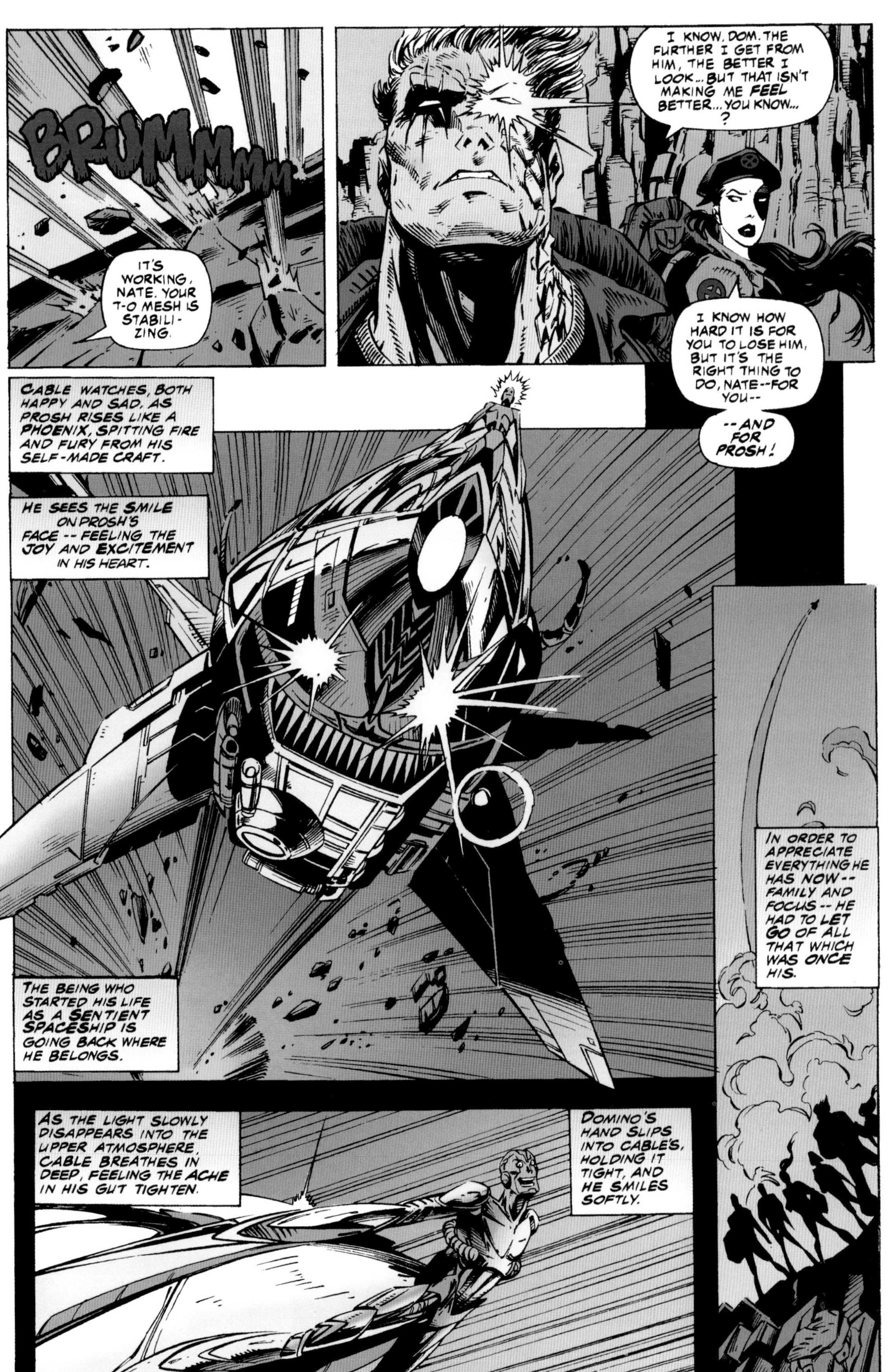
BRUMMMMM
IT'S WORKING, NATE. YOUR T-O MESH IS STABILI-ZING.
I KNOW, DOM. THE FURTHER I GET FROM HIM, THE BETTER I LOOK... BUT THAT ISN'T MAKING ME FEEL BETTER... YOU KNOW... ?
I KNOW HOW HARD IT IS FOR YOU TO LOSE HIM, BUT IT'S THE RIGHT THING TO DO, NATE--FOR YOU--
--AND FOR PROSH!
CABLE WATCHES, BOTH HAPPY AND SAD, AS PROSH RISES LIKE A PHOENIX, SPITTING FIRE AND FURY FROM HIS SELF-MADE CRAFT.
HE SEES THE SMILE ON PROSH'S FACE -- FEELING THE JOY AND EXCITEMENT IN HIS HEART.
THE BEING WHO STARTED HIS LIFE AS A SENTIENT SPACESHIP IS GOING BACK WHERE HE BELONGS.
IN ORDER TO APPRECIATE EVERYTHING HE HAS NOW -- FAMILY AND FOCUS -- HE HAD TO LET GO OF ALL THAT WHICH WAS ONCE HIS.
AS THE LIGHT SLOWLY DISAPPEARS INTO THE UPPER ATMOSPHERE, CABLE BREATHES IN DEEP, FEELING THE ACHE IN HIS GUT TIGHTEN.
DOMINO'S HAND SLIPS INTO CABLE'S, HOLDING IT TIGHT, AND HE SMILES SOFTLY.

IT IS ONE OF THE HARDEST THINGS THE MAN CALLED CABLE HAS EVER HAD TO DO SINCE COMING TO THIS TIME.
YOU GOING TO BE OKAY WITH THIS?
THE FIRST WAS ADMITTING HOW MUCH HE NEEDED THIS RAG-TAG FAMILY TO BEGIN WITH.
YEAH, DOM...
...I AM.
AND IT WAS A HOLLOW COMPUTER VOICE CALLED THE PROFESSOR WHO WAS THERE FOR HIM BOTH TIMES.
SO IN ALL WAYS, THEY HAVE COME FULL-CIRCLE--
--AND EACH GIVEN HOPE TO THE OTHER.
HE HELPED TEACH ME... THAT I AM-- I ALWAYS WAS-- MORE THAN METAL--
--I'M BLOOD, TOO.
AND I HAVE BLOOD AGAIN. I HAVE A FAMILY AGAIN.
I HAVE A LIFE.
LET'S START LIVING IT...

FINE BY ALL OF US. BUT WHERE'RE WE GONNA GO TO DO IT?
FUNNY YOU SHOULD ASK, SAMMY...
NEXT: A NEW HQ!! NEW BEGINNINGS! AND THE RETURN OF AN OLD FRIEND...

TONY DANIEL
-w-
KEVIN CONRAD
94
MASON

MARVEL COMICS
NOV • 40
X-MEN
X-FORCE
APPROVED BY THE COMICS CODE AUTHORITY
TONY DANIEL -w- KEVIN CONRAD '94
MADNESS AND MURDER!

MANHATTAN.
NEW YORK POLICE DEPARTMENT DETECTIVE JOSÉ HIDALSO HAS TRACKED A MURDER SUSPECT--
--INTO THE UNDERLYING NETWORK OF TUNNELS WHICH EXIST DEEP BENEATH THE CITY STREETS.
SINCE THIS SUSPECT IS ALSO A MUTANT, BORN WITH SUPERHUMAN ABILITIES...
I HATE SEWER JOBS.
KEEP 'EM ZIPPED, RASSITANO.
...HIDALGO ASKED FOR SOME VERY SPECIAL ASSISTANCE TO JOIN HIM.
DON'T WORRY ABOUT IT TOO MUCH,
THE YOUNG WOMAN WE'RE SEARCHING FOR HAS PROBABLY BEEN AWARE OF OUR PRESENCE IN THE TUNNELS SINCE WE FIRST CAME IN!
CODE: BLUE-- THE NYPD'S SUPERHUMAN TASK FORCE.
I HATE SPANDEX WHO HAVE ENHANCED SENSES, TOO!
THEIR MEMBERS, IN-CLUDING STONE, RASSITANO AND RUIZ, ARE CONSIDERED EITHER THE BEST THE CITY HAS TO OFFER--
--OR THE CRAZIEST!
FOR THIS ASSIGNMENT, HIDALGO SUSPECTS THE LATTER TO BE TRUE, AND PRAYS THE FORMER WILL BE AS WELL.
LUCIA CALLASANTOS DISAPPEARED FOUR YEARS AGO--AFTER ALL THE BAD THINGS STARTED GOING DOWN.
SHE CALLS HERSELF THORNN NOW--
--AN OUTLAW WHO USED TO BE A MEMBER OF A GROUP OF MUTANT OUTCASTS WHO LIVED IN THESE TUNNELS UNTIL RECENTLY.*
SHE WAS BEAUTIFUL... HAD EVERYTHING GOING FOR HER. AND IT ALL TURNED OUT LIKE THIS... IN A DANK, DARK SEWER.
*THE MORLOCKS.--BOB

SHE WAS SPOTTED A COUPLE OF WEEKS AGO DURING A BIT OF A SKIRMISH IN CENTRAL PARK.*
I KNOW IT MIGHT BE A REAL LONG SHOT TO EXPECT TO FIND HER HERE--
--BUT AFTER WORKING ON THIS CASE FOR SO LONG, I'LL GRASP AT ANY STRAWS I CAN!
*AS SEEN IN CABLE #15.--BOB
WE CAME WITH THE BEST MUTANT-SCANNING EQUIPMENT AVAILABLE.
IF THE PERP'S HERE, HIDALGO, WE'LL FIND HER.
TRUTH TO TELL, STONE...
...I'M MORE WORRIED ABOUT HER FINDING US FIRST!
CODE
IF WISHES WERE FISHES.
WE GOT A MUTAGENIC TRACKING LOCK.
RUIZ, GET A PERIMETER SWEEP STARTED. I GOT MOVEMENT--!
FROM WHICH DIRECTION, LUTE?
FROM RIGHT ABOVE YOU!!
FACHOW
SONOVA--! SHE CAME OUTTA NOWHERE!
HOW CAN ANYONE MOVE THAT FAST?!
FACHOW

THIPP
THIPP
GYAAAAGHNK-!
LUCIA.
FOR THE MURDERS OF CAROLINA, MATTEO AND MARCELLA CALLASANTOS!
YOU'RE UNDER ARREST.
JOSE--? 'ZAT YOU--? HURRGGHH-- YOU--TRANKED ME--?!
I DIDN' KILL MY FAMILY!! SHE DID!!
TRANQUILIZED WITH ENOUGH JUICE TO KNOCK OUT AN ELE-PHANT, THORNN.
WHUD-- ARRESSED-- FOR--?
THE ANAESTHETIC SEEPS THROUGH HER BLOOD AND THORNN FALLS UNCONSCIOUS.
HIDALGO SAYS NOTHING AS CODE: BLUE CARRIES HER INTO THEIR EVAC CHOPPER--
--AND HEADS TOWARDS THE BRONX PRECINCT HOUSE WHERE SHE'LL BE DETAINED.
BUT HE CAN'T STOP THINKING ABOUT THE FEELINGS HE ONCE HAD FOR THIS GIRL--
--AND THE LOOK OF BETRAYAL IN HER EYES WHEN SHE PROCLAIMED HER INNOCENCE. "SHE DID!" SHE CRIED.
AND WHO ELSE COULD LUCIA HAVE MEANT, BUT HER?

CANNONBALL. WARPATH. SIRYN. RICTOR. SHATTERSTAR. BOOMER. THEY CALL THEMSELVES X-FORCE.
THEY ARE A BAND OF YOUNG, OUTLAW MUTANTS DETERMINED TO FIGHT FOR A DREAM OF CO-EXISTENCE BETWEEN THEIR KIND AND HUMANS.
HAVING TAKEN A LOOK AT THEIR NEW BASE OF OPERATIONS, THEIR FEELINGS ABOUT THIS NEW HOME ARE BEING SUCCINCTLY SUMMED UP--
YOU GOTTA BE KIDDIN'-?!

NOPE, BOOMER, WE'RE NOT.
WELCOME TO OUR NEW HQ --
-- THE FORMER UNDERGROUND BASE OF THE ASSASSIN FOR HIRE KNOWN AS ARCADE --
DOMINO... YOU AN' CABLE WANT US TA SHACK UP IN A PLACE THAT WAS MADE SO PEOPLE COULD BE KILLED FOR FUN AN' PROFIT?
STAN LEE PRESENTS
HOLDING ON
BROUGHT TO YOU BY
FABIAN NICIEZA THE RINGLEADER
TONY DANIEL THE JUGGLER
CONRAD 1-18, 21, 22 TOWNSEND 19, 20 THE HUMAN PRETZELS

-MURDERWORLD!

THE SITE IS ISOLATED, SAM, YET RIGHT ABOVE US IS NEW YORK CITY!

WE HAVE ACCESS NOT ONLY TO ALL KINDS OF SOPHISTICATED EQUIPMENT, BUT ALSO TO THE REAL WORLD--

--AND A CHANCE FOR LIVES OUTSIDE OF BEING IN X-FORCE!

SOUNDS SPLENDID, DOM.

I EVEN SAW A PLANT SHOP A FEW BLOCKS AWAY WHERE I'D LOVE T'WORK--

--BUT HOW DID YE MANAGE T'CONVINCE ARCADE T'SELL US THE PROPERTY?

CHRIS ELIOPOULOS- THE BARKER
MARIE JAVINS- THE BEARDED LADY
(JUST KIDDING!)
BOB HARRAS- THE ELEPHANT TRAINER
TOM DEFALCO- THE ELEPHANT

WE DO NOT NEED TO BARTER WITH A COWARD!
WE HAVE TAKEN THIS FACILITY FROM HIM AND SHALL SPIT IN HIS FACE SHOULD HE TRY TO TAKE IT BACK!

UHM... PRETTY MUCH WHAT HE SAID, SIRYN.
OKAY, DOM, AH GUESS IT DOES MAKE SENSE--
--WITH THE KINDA LOGIC THIS GROUP EMPLOYS, AT ANY RATE--
--TO MAKE USE OF A PLACE LIKE THIS.
AH MEAN, IT IS AN ELABORATE FACILITY. COMMUNICATIONS CENTER, LIVIN' QUARTERS, MATERIAL WE CAN ADAPT INTO TRAININ' EQUIPMENT... THE WHOLE WORKS!
MURDERWOR

BUT THE NAME HAS GOTTA GO!

PLASMA BOMB SIGNAGE COMPANY, PRESIDENT BOOMER SPEAKING.
HOW MAY I HELP YOU?
PHOOON

SKACHOW!
SO NOW ALL WE GOTTA DO IS COME UP WITH A NEW NAME, HUH?
I SUGGEST "BOOMERVILLE."

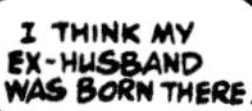
I THINK MY EX-HUSBAND WAS BORN THERE.
HE CAME FROM A LONG LINE OF INBRED COUSINS.
HERE'S THE MAIN CONTROL ROOM.
WE STILL HAVE SOME WORK TO DO HERE. REROUTING PROGRAMS, WIRING NEW CONDUITS, STUFF LIKE THAT.

WILL THAT STOP ARCADE'S GRINNIN' FACE FROM AP-PEARIN' ON A SCREEN EVERY TIME WE PUSH A BUTTON?
GOD, I HOPE SO.
ANYWAY, I WANTED TO SHOW YOU A SCHEMATIC OF THE FACILITY--

--BUT SINCE I HAVEN'T HAD A CHANCE TO REROUTE THE HOLOGRAPHIC RELAYS--

--WE'RE GOING TO HAVE TO GET PRIMITIVE AND SCROLL THE DATA ON-SCREEN.
SIGH
EVERYTHING'S A TRADE-OFF IN LIFE, GANG.
BUT AT LEAST THIS PLACE HAS RUNNING WATER!
SNAPP!

PRETTY COOL, HOW THE PLACE WAS BUILT UNDER AN ABANDONED AMUSEMENT PARK.

AND A *LANDFILL* TO THE WEST.

CRAK!

WELL, WHAT'S ABOVE NOT-WITHSTANDING, WHAT'S *BELOW* IS *PERFECT.*

FUSION GENERATORS UNDER THE LINK-TUNNEL, A THREE LEVEL MODULE FOR *VERY* SPACIOUS LIVING QUARTERS--

--A FOUR LEVEL MODULE FOR TRAINING AND EQUIPMENT--

--SEVERAL ACCESS TUNNELS TO THE SURFACE, A PNEUMATIC TRAM-LINE INTO *MANHATTAN*--
--AND A VEHICLE EXIT INTO THE *EAST RIVER.*
AND WHAT A *ROMANTIC* VIEW OF *RYKER'S ISLAND*
WE LL GET ON TAKE-OFF AN' LANDIN'!
WELL, THE WAY *THIS* OUTFIT OPERATES, WE'LL END UP *LIVING* THERE EVENTUALLY, SO FAMILIARIZING OURSELVES WITH THE PLACE WOULDN'T HURT!

WE'RE STILL UNDERGROUND, BUT AT LEAST NOW WE'RE AIR-CONDITIONED AND OUT OF THAT BLOODY *ARIZONA* HEAT!
WAS OUR PREVIOUS HOME CONSIDERED *HOT* BY EARTH STANDARDS?-HUMPH-
DOM, KEEP TALKING, *QUICK!*
BEFORE SHATTY STARTS TELLIN' US ANOTHER STORY ABOUT HOW *ROUGH* IT WAS ON *HIS* HOMEWORLD!

GOOD POINT.
OKAY, OKAY, FORGETTING THE FUNKY LIFE-SIZED PINBALL MACHINE WE CAN PLAY--
-- I'D RATHER TALK ABOUT THE *REAL LIFE* YOU CAN ALL HAVE NOW.
COLLEGES ALL AROUND: EMPIRE STATE, COLUMBIA, ST. JOHNS-- JOBS TO BE HAD. WE CAN WATCH THE METS LOSE AT SHEA, THE RANGERS HOIST THEIR NEXT CUP--
ENOUGH-- AH THINK YOU'VE CONVINCED US.
THE GOOD OUTWEIGHS THE BAD.
BUT PART'A ME MIGHT *ALWAYS* FEEL WEIRD KNOWIN' WE'RE LIVIN' IN A PLACE WHERE OUR FRIENDS WERE ALMOST *KILLED*.
IF IT DOESN'T WORK OUT IN THE LONG RUN, SAM, THEN WE'LL JUST BUG OUT. *NATE* HAS NO PROBLEM WITH THAT.
FAIR ENOUGH.
AN' SPEAKIN' OF *CABLE*-- WHERE'S HE BEEN?

HE HAD *SOME BUSINESS* TO DEAL WITH. HE WANTED TO MEET IN THE MAIN LOUNGE TO TALK ABOUT IT AFTER OUR LITTLE TOUR.
SKKRICHCH
WE DON'T EVEN GET TO *UNPACK* BEFORE GOIN' T'KICK SOMEONE'S BUTT IN?
SHEEESH! SOME THINGS NEVER CHANGE, HUH?

KRYEEEEENKK
NOPE...

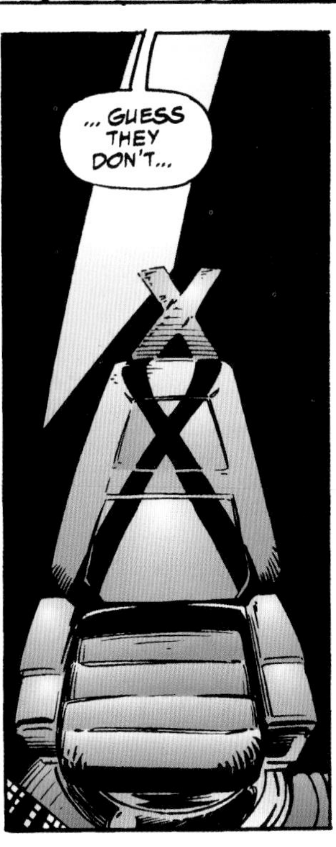
...GUESS THEY DON'T...

EARLY EVENING IN THE BRONX...
--HERE AT THE FORTY-FOURTH PRECINCT STATION HOUSE, SUE, AS WORD HAS SPREAD THAT A MUTANT HAS BEEN ARRESTED--
--FOR A HORRIBLE CRIME THAT HAD REMAINED UNSOLVED FOR SEVERAL YEARS--
--THE APPARENTLY SYSTEMATIC MURDER OF AN ENTIRE FAMILY WHO LIVED IN THIS AREA.
A GROWING CROWD OF PEOPLE HAS GATHERED HERE--
--LED BY MEMBERS OF THE ANTI-MUTANT, HUMAN RIGHTS ORGANIZATION KNOWN AS THE FRIENDS OF HUMANITY.
THE POLICE HAVE NOT ISSUED A STATEMENT AS OF YET, AND THE MOOD OF THE PEOPLE GROWS RESTLESS--
--AS THEY ASK THEMSELVES, WHAT KIND OF MONSTERS ARE LIVING NEXT DOOR TO US? BACK TO YOU, SUE.
TRIED AND CONVICTED ALREADY, LUCIA.
I HOPE IT'S NOT JUST BECAUSE YOU'RE A MUTANT.
I PRAY THE PEOPLE DOWN THERE ARE ANGRIER ABOUT WHAT HAPPENED TO YOUR MOTHER, BROTHER AND SISTER--
--THAN THEY ARE ABOUT THE FUR ON YOUR SKIN.
WHATTAYOU THINK THE ODDS OF THAT, ARE, JOSÉ?
ALL I KNOW IS THAT I KNEW YOU WHEN, LUCIA CALLASANTOS!
BEFORE YOU MUTATED--BEFORE YOU RAN AWAY!
I KNEW YOU AS YOUR FAMILY DIED OFF ONE BY ONE--
--AND WHEN I BECAME A COP, I SWORE I WAS GOING TO DIG-UP THE TRUTH ABOUT THEIR DEATHS!

THAT'S WHAT IT'S ABOUT, FOR YOU, JOSÉ?
A COP JUST DOING HIS JOB?
WELL, YOU GOT ME. ONE MORE LOUSY HUMAN-KILLING *MUTIE* BROUGHT TO JUSTICE, HUH?

LUCIA, WHEN WE WERE KIDS... YOU KNEW HOW I FELT ABOUT YOU...
...YOU *KNOW* HOW MUCH I CARED FOR YOU.
WHEN YOU RAN AWAY... YOU TOOK MY *HEART* WITH YOU.

I HAVE TO KNOW... IS THE GIRL I LOVED A *COLD-BLOODED KILLER*?

I GET ONE PHONE CALL, DON'T I?

YEAH, LUCIA... YOU GET ONE PHONE CALL.

AS IF ANY *LAWYER* IN THIS CITY IS GOING TO BE ABLE TO SAVE YOU NOW...

MUTIES LEAVE EARTH!

--AS THE SCENE HERE GROWS PROGRESSIVELY MORE CONFRONTATIONAL, MICHELLE--
--WE WAIT AND WONDER, JUST HOW MUCH MORE PRESSURE WILL THE FRIENDS OF HUMANITY HAVE TO BRING ON THE SITUATION--
--BEFORE THE POLICE RELEASE THE IDENTITY OF THIS MUTANT MURDER SUSPECT?
GRAYDON CREED, THE FOUNDER OF THE FRIENDS, SMILES...
...KNOWING HIS ORGANIZATION IS DOING WHAT HE ALWAYS INTENDED IT TO DO...
...TO PUSH...TO CONFRONT...TO POINT OUT AT EVERY OPPORTUNITY THE DANGER THIS NEW SPECIES OF MAN REPRESENTS...
...TO SHOW EVERYONE THE THREAT MUTANTS TRULY ARE.
--WITH THIS JUST RELEASED, THE SUSPECT IS NAMED--
--LUCIA CALLASANTOS, WHOSE MOTHER, BROTHER AND SISTER WERE ALL--
ECTRONIC
SOMEWHERE IN NEW YORK, A LONE FIGURE STOPS...
...AND THEN HASTENS INTO THE SHADOWS.
THIS MUG SHOT WAS RELEASED, SHOWING QUITE CLEARLY THE SUSPECT IS A MUTANT.
WESTCHESTER. THE XAVIER INSTITUTE.
SHOULD WE CONSIDER A PLAN OF ACTION, PROFESSOR?
NO, HANK. THE X-MEN NEEDN'T GET INVOLVED JUST YET.
CABLE HAS ALREADY CALLED ME. THIS INVOLVES HIS FORMER STUDENT, FERAL.
THE SUSPECT'S SISTER--ANOTHER MUTANT CALLED FERAL--
--WAS SIGHTED WITH HER REBEL FACTION, X-FORCE--
--AT THE WORLD TRADE CENTER INCIDENT, MONTHS AGO.
WHETHER A LINK EXISTS BETWEEN THE MURDERS AND X-FORCE REMAINS UNKOWN.
OF COURSE. LINK US ALL TOGETHER BECAUSE WE'RE MUTANTS. TYPICAL MEDIA STEREOTYPE.

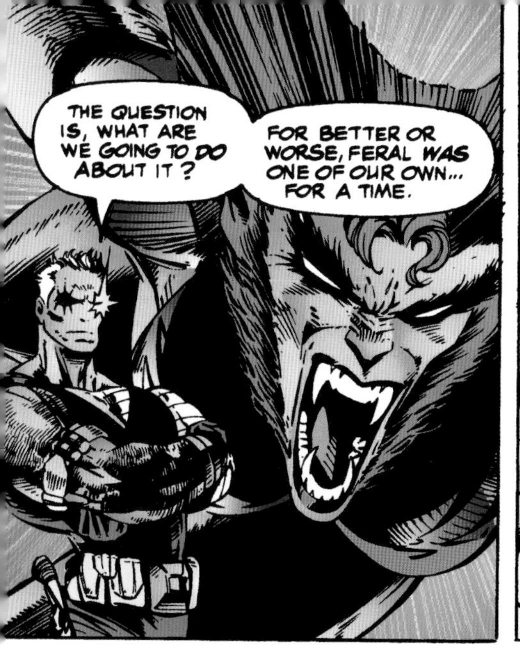
THE QUESTION IS, WHAT ARE WE GOING TO DO ABOUT IT?
FOR BETTER OR WORSE, FERAL WAS ONE OF OUR OWN... FOR A TIME.

WE HAVE A RESPONSIBILITY.
NOT TO FERAL, SIR.

AH'D SAY WE HAVE MORE OF A RESPONSIBILITY TA THE MEMORIES OF THE PEOPLE FERAL OR HER SISTER MAY'VE MURDERED!
LET THORNN STAND TRIAL. IF SHE'S GUILTY, SHE'LL GO TA JAIL.

FAIR ENOUGH, SAMMY. BUT THE WAY PEOPLE FEEL ABOUT MUTANTS BEGGARS THE QUESTION...
...CAN SHE EVEN GET A FAIR TRIAL AT THIS POINT?

AH FELT FERAL'S CLAWS RIP THROUGH ME, JIMMY. *
AH KNOW WHAT SHE'S CAPABLE A' DOIN'.

X-FORCE #2 --BOB
WHAT'S TA SAY HER SISTER'S ANY DIFFERENT?
WHAT ABOUT THE NOTION OF INNOCENT UNTIL PROVEN GUILTY, SAM--
--OR ARE WE JUST TOSSING THAT OUT THE WINDOW BE-CAUSE YOU DON'T LIKE FERAL OR THORNN?
SOMETHING ABOUT THIS FEELS WRONG. AND I WANT TO FIND OUT WHAT.
AND I WANT TO FIND OUT NOW.

MORNING IN THE SOUTH BRONX.
THE 44TH PRECINCT.
THE FRIENDS OF HUMANITY STAYED THROUGH THE NIGHT.
THE LOCAL RESIDENTS BROUGHT OUT COFFEE AND DONUTS FOR THEM AS THE SUN CAME UP.
THIS PART OF THE CITY HAS ALWAYS BEEN ON THE OTHER SIDE OF THE CANYON BETWEEN THE HAVES AND HAVE-NOTS.
YOU SURE YOU KNOW WHAT WE'RE DOIN' HERE?
IF JUST ONE'A THESE "FRIENDS" RECOGNIZES US--
THORNN MADE HER PHONE CALL.
IT WAS TO ME.
I'M HER LAWYER NOW.
BUT YOU AIN'T A LAWYER!
"US VERSUS THEM" HAS A NEW TWIST NOW. IT HAS BECOME THE RALLYING CRY OF HUMANS VERSUS MUTANTS...
...ECHOING ACROSS THE GENETIC GAP BETWEEN THE PAST AND THE FUTURE.
HARVARD. CLASS OF EIGHTY-EIGHT.
PASSED THE NEW YORK BAR EXAM A YEAR LATER. IT WAS PRETTY EASY.
N.Y. STATE BAR LICENSE
SUMMERS, NATHAN C.
SEE, SAM? I'M STILL FULL OF SURPRISES.
44th
KILL
MUTIE'S INHUMAN

MR. SUMMERS, MR. GUTHRIE-- THIS WAY.
YOUR CLIENT IS WAITING FOR YOU.
LUCIA. HOW ARE YOU?
WHAT DO YOU THINK, CABLE?
I DON'T KNOW. YOU CALLED. I CAME.
NOW GIVE ME ONE REASON WHY WE SHOULD HELP YOU.
SIMPLE. I DIDN'T KILL MY FAMILY.
SAYIN' IT DON'T MEAN MUCH, CONSIDERING YOUR TRACK RECORD, GIRL!
YOU GOT A PROBLEM WITH MY SISTER, CANNONBALL, TAKE IT UP WITH HER!
WE MAY ALL SOON GET THE CHANCE, LUCIA.
I HAVE IT ON GOOD AUTHORITY THAT FERAL IS BACK IN MANHATTAN.
TELL ME. DID SHE COME BACK LOOKING TO KILL YOU?
IS SHE HAPPY YOU WERE ARRESTED--
--OR IS SHE TERRIFIED YOU'LL TALK?
AND IF YOU DID TALK, LUCIA... WHAT WOULD YOU HAVE TO SAY?

YOU REALLY WANNA KNOW, CABLE ?
YOU'RE WORRIED. AREN'T YOU, BIG MAN ?
YOU'RE AFRAID THAT FERAL'S FAR WORSE THAN ANYTHING YOU EVER DREAMED.
LOOKS LIKE THE GENERAL DIDN'T KNOW HIS TROOPS AS WELL AS HE THOUGHT. ONE OF 'EM WENT BAD, AND THAT HURTS. DON'T IT, CABLE ?
I'VE MADE MISTAKES BEFORE, THORNN. AND I'LL MAKE 'EM AGAIN.
BUT A MAN RIGHTS HIS OWN WRONGS.
NOW TELL ME... EVERYTHING.
LATER...
HIDALGO.
MR. SUMMERS, I'VE BEEN EXPECTING YOU.
SO I HEAR. YOU KNOW LUCIA IS INNOCENT, DON'T YOU ?
MAYBE I DO, MAYBE I DON'T.
LET A JURY DECIDE.
YOU DON'T WANT A VERDICT, DETECTIVE. YOU WANT THE TRUTH.
I CAN GET THAT FOR YOU.
YOU KNOW SO MUCH, MR. SUMMERS...
...TELL ME... YOU A MIND-READER ?
MAYBE I AM. MAYBE I'M NOT.
OFF THE RECORD. I CAN GIVE YOU MARIA CALLASANTOS. THE TRUTH WILL COME OUT.
AND HOW MIGHT YOU BE ABLE TO SUPPLY ME WITH THAT INDIVIDUAL ?
OFF THE RECORD, OF COURSE... CABLE...

IN VIEW OF THE SITUATION AT THE 44TH, A DECISION IS MADE TO RELOCATE THORNN TO THE MORE SECURE FACILITIES AT RYKER'S ISLAND.
TO AVOID ANTI-MUTANT HYSTERIA, HIDALGO HAD THE TRANSPORT ARRANGED AND KEPT CODE: BLUE OFF THE ASSIGNMENT.
BUT OTHER SOURCES OUTSIDE THE DEPARTMENT ALSO CUT SOME DEALS. DOCUMENTS WERE REVEALED, PHOTOS SHOWN.
BLACKMAIL... THE FRIENDS OF HUMANITY'S SPECIALTY... AND THUS, TWO SPECIFIC MEN SERVE AS DRIVERS...
WHERE'S THE RENDEZVOUS SET UP FOR?
OFF THE BRUCKNER IN SOUNDVIEW PARK.
WE CLAIM A PSYCHO-MUTANT TRIED ESCAPING --
-- AND WAS KILLED IN THE ATTEMPT.
"ONE LESS MUTIE SCUM RUINING THE LIVES OF DECENT HUMANS. ANOTHER STEP FORWARD FOR THE FRIENDS OF HUMANITY!"
THEY'RE MAKIN' THE DETOUR. CABLE WAS RIGHT. THORNN WAS NEVER GONNA MAKE IT TO RYKER'S.
READY, 'STAR?
ON MY WORLD, SUCH VEHICLES PERFORM AIRBORNE MANEUVERS.
YEAH, WELL, HERE YOU JUST GOTTA --
-- IMPROVISE!
VRRRAAAAAANNNNN
WHAT THE--?
MUTIES!

THEY'RE PICKING UP SPEED, RIC. THEY'RE GETTING AWAY!
DID YOU GET A LOOK AT THOSE JOKERS...
VRRRAAAANNNN
...IF THOSE GUYS ARE COPS, I'M CABLE'S MOTHER!
WE GOTTA GET THORNN OUTTA THERE BEFORE THAT VAN REACHES THE RENDEZVOUS WITH THE FRIENDS --
--OR ELSE SHE AND HIDALGO ARE AS GOOD AS DEAD!
I KNOW, SAM.
I GUESS WE'LL JUST HAVE TO DEAL WITH THEM AS GENTLY AS THEY WERE GOING TO DEAL WITH THORNN, EH?
HE SAYS WHILE HE'S DRIVIN' A CAR WITH ENOUGH FIREPOWER TO LEVEL MANHATTAN!
VRUMMMMM

RICTOR, YOU'RE UP NEXT. YOU KNOW WHAT TO DO.
YEAH, CABLE, I GOTCHA. GENTLE.
JUST LIKE I DID IN MEMPHIS A FEW WEEKS BACK--*
--LOW-LEVEL VIBE-QUAKE--
*ISSUE #35.--BOB
PWOOOF
--TAKE OUT THE TIRE, THEY'LL COME TO A QUICK STOP.
WE BEEN HIT! THEY'RE ON TO US!
I GOTTA PULL OVER!
NO! I'LL TAKE 'EM OUT! YOU JUST KEEP YOUR EYES ON THE--
SKAKRASHKKKT

VERY STOPPABLE OBJECT, MEET VERY IMMOVABLE FORCE.
PLEASED TO MEET YOU.
BOTH F.O.H. PLANTS ARE DOWN, CABLE. MOVE IN.
FACHOW!
HIDALGO -- THORNN--LET'S ROLL.
THIS WAS YOUR IDEA OF A PRE-PLANNED, NON-VIOLENT EXTRACTION?
N.Y.P.D.
UNAVOIDABLE PROBLEM. TWO OF NEW YORK'S FINEST WERE SUBSTITUTED WITH MEMBERS OF THE FRIENDS OF HUMANITY.
WE HAVE TO GET TO THE MEETING SITE BEFORE ANY FRIENDS CAN TRACK US.
WHAT'S GOIN' ON HERE?
WHY ARE YOU FREEING ME?
CHIKK
SNIPP
WE WANT TO FIND OUT THE TRUTH ONCE AND FOR ALL, THORNN.
--AND WE'RE GOING TO THE ONE PLACE--
--TO SEE THE ONE PERSON--
--WHO'LL HELP US GET TO THE BOTTOM OF THIS SAD MESS.
OH NO -- POR EL AMOR DE DIOS--
--DON'T DO THIS TO ME...

JOSÉ, IT'S THE BUILDING WHERE WE GREW UP.
IT'S BEEN YEARS. LOOK AT THIS PLACE-- IT'S ALL GONE--
--THERE'S NO ONE HERE...
ACTUALLY, LUCIA, IF THINGS WENT ACCORDING TO PLAN--
--AND OUR OUTSIDE CONTACT DID HER JOB RIGHT--
--THERE SHOULD BE ONE PERSON HERE.
YOU?!
ME, SISTER.
FERAL IS HERE.
TRICKED INTO COMIN' HERE. SET UP BY YOU.
STINKIN' MEAT! I HATE YOU ALL!
BUT YOU WANT THE TRUTH 'BOUT WHAT HAPPENED?
YOU'RE GONNA HAVETA TEAR IT OUTTA ME!
WHO WANTS TO GO FIRST?
NEXT
THE MYSTERY REVEALED-- AND THE ANSWERS WILL SHOCK YOU!!

MARVEL COMICS
DEC 41
X-MEN
X-FORCE
APPROVED BY THE COMICS CODE AUTHORITY
TONY DANIEL

THE FUN HOUSE
~A TALE OF DECEPTION AND DEATH~
THE SOUTH BRONX...
THERE ARE GHOSTS AT PLAY IN THE SHADOWS ABOUT THEM.
THIS ABANDONED TENEMENT BUILDING HOLDS THE ANSWERS TO A LONG-AGO TRAGIC MYSTERY THAT THEY SEEK TO UNRAVEL.
BUT FOR THE MUTANT MEMBERS OF X-FORCE, CANNONBALL AND SHATTER-STAR, THE FORMER MORLOCK THORNN AS WELL AS THEIR NEW-FOUND ALLY NEW YORK CITY POLICE, DETECTIVE JOSE HIDALGO--
--GHOSTS ALSO HAUNT THEIR MEMORIES.
STAN LEE Presents
An X-FORCE Adventure!
Brought To You By:
FABIAN NICIEZA - WRITER
TONY DANIEL - PENCILER
KEVIN CONRAD - INKER
ELIOPOULOS & OAKLEY - LETTERERS
MARIE JAVINS - COLORIST
BOB HARRAS - EDITOR
TOM DEFALCO - EDITOR IN CHIEF

FOR AS THEY SYSTEMATICALLY CONDUCT AN INTERIOR SEARCH OF THE TENEMENT--
--ALL FOUR SEE THE CRUMBLED RUINS AROUND THEM--
--BITS AND PIECES OF SOMEONE THEY ONCE CALLED FRIEND...
WHY? WE WOULD BE WELL SERVED TO FIND THE TRAITOR, FERAL--
--GUT HER AND BE DONE WITH THIS!
SHATTERSTAR, SLOW IT DOWN, BUDDY...
...STOP GOIN' AHEAD OF THE PACK.
STAR, AH KNOW HOW YOU FEEL ABOUT HER!
FERAL FOOLED THE LOT O' US--
--BUT SHE DID EVEN MORE TA ME, REMEMBER? SHE NEARLY KILLED ME!
BUT-- NO MATTER WHAT-- WE AIN'T HERE TA KILL HER!
WE JUST WANNA FIND OUT THE TRUTH ABOUT WHAT REALLY HAPPENED TO HER AN' THORNN'S FAMILY--
--AN' GUILTY OR INNOCENT, TRY AN' FIND A WAY TA HELP THEM BOTH!

YOU DON'T THINK THAT'S GOING TO HAPPEN, DO YOU, KID?
NO, JOSÉ... I DON'T.
THE GIRL I USED TO KNOW-- THE GIRL YOU WERE, LUCIA CALLASANTOS --HAD A LOT OF HOPE INSIDE HER HEART.
IS THERE ANY LEFT INSIDE THE MUTANT NAMED THORNN?
HOPE LEFT ME A LONG TIME AGO, STAMPED OUT SO HARD THAT I CAN BARELY REMEMBER WHAT IT FELT LIKE.
LOOK, JOSÉ -- REMEMBER. THIS IS WHERE MY SISTER DIED! THIS IS WHERE IT BEGAN!
CAROLINA...
I TOLD MARIA TO WATCH HER FOR FIVE MINUTES.
I HAD SEEN YOU AN' YOUR FRIENDS OUT-SIDE, I WANTED TO PLAY WITH YOU.
T-THEN WE HEARD HER SCREAM. W-WE ALL RAN INSIDE.
I DON'T KNOW-- I NEVER REALLY FOUND OUT--
--DID CAROLINA FALL DOWN THE STAIRS--
--OR WAS SHE PUSHED?

CHIFF
PICHKK
HUH--? PLASTER?
X-FORCE, WATCH OUT--
--I GOT MOVEMENT!
FACHOW
FACHOW
JOSÉ--NO! BEHIND YOU--!!
HASHSSHSHSSS
LONG TIME, HERMANA MIA.
ALL I'M DOIN', LUCIA, IS WHAT I ALWAYS DONE--
--FINDIN' A WAY TO SURVIVE!
MARIA--?!
LET GO OF HIM, LITTLE SISTER!
DON'T DO THIS--PLEASE--!
MARIA...

AND JUST OUTSIDE THE TENEMENT...
...IN X-FORCE'S CONCEALED TRACKER...
CABLE, SHE GOT THE JUMP ON US! SHE TOOK HIDALGO HOSTAGE.
JUST GREAT!
YOU WERE SENT IN THERE TO FLUSH HER OUT--
--AND INSTEAD, FERAL'S GOING TO PICK YOU OFF ONE AT A TIME!
SKAKRA
SOUNDS LIKE YOU TRAINED HER TOO WELL, DOESN'T IT, NATE?
HEY, THE COP WAS SO GUNG-HO TO GO IN THERE, DOMINO, WHAT COULD WE HAVE DONE?
I MEAN, HE WAS OUR ALIBI FOR BUSTIN' THORNN OUTTA POLICE CUSTODY!
HOO. I DUNNO, MAYBE SAY "NO," RICTOR?
WE NEED HIDALGO ALIVE AFTER ALL THIS IS DONE.
HIDALGO HAD TO GO IN-- HE'S DOING HIS JOB. AND WE'RE DOING OURS!
DO YOU NEED ANY ADDITIONAL SUPPORT IN THERE, SAM?
NO, SIR, WE CAN HANDLE IT, BUT...
...MAYBE SIRYN SHOULD GO AIR-BORNE IN CASE FERAL TRIES GETTIN' AWAY OVER THE ROOFTOPS.
DONE.
SO AH HEAR.
THE OTHERS ARE SPREADING OUT TO COVER THE ENTIRE PERIMETER.
STAY IN TOUCH, SAM.
IF NECESSARY, WE CAN TAKE THE WHOLE BUILDING DOWN IN FIVE SECONDS.

KRAKAKOOM!
AND AGAIN I SAY THAT WHERE SOMEONE LIKE FERAL IS CONCERNED--
--THERE IS ONLY ONE SOLUTION.
AN' WE CAN BLAST IT DOWN IN TWO--
--BUT THAT AIN'T GONNA SOLVE OUR PROBLEMS.
THERE'S ALWAYS MORE'N THAT, 'STAR.
BAD SEED THAT SHE IS, FERAL WAS STILL FAMILY, IN A WAY.
"AN' THE WAY AH WAS RAISED, YOU ALWAYS TRY TO DO RIGHT BY YOUR FAMILY.
"AH JUST HOPE HIDALGO'S OKAY."
NYPD
UHHHN
IS THAT YOUR ANSWER, NIÑA?
TRY TO HURT THE PEOPLE WHO WANT TO HELP YOU?
HELP ME, JOSE?! SURE!
YOU JUS' WANNA MAKE YOUR MUTIE COLLAR AN' GETCHOU FACE ON THE FRONT PAGE OF THE POST!
HAVEN'T CHANGED A BIT, HAVE YOU, MARIA?
TIENES TANTA MALDAD ENCIMA, NO?
EVIL INSIDE AN' OUT.

... JUS' SOMETIMES...
... SOMETIMES...
... IT ALL GETS TOO MUCH, Y' KNOW?
NAAAH, NOT EVIL, JOSÉ...
CAROLINA DIED FALLING DOWN THE STAIRS.
YOUR BROTHER, MATTEO, FELL OFF THE ROOF. TWO ACCIDENTAL DEATHS --
-- STATISTICALLY POSSIBLE, BUT IT RAISED EYEBROWS, DIDN'T IT, MARIA?
THEN YOUR MOTHER DIED WHEN YOU WERE FIFTEEN, AND NO ONE THOUGHT THAT WAS AN ACCIDENT.
POLICE LINE: DO N
OT CROSS
AND THAT'S JUST ABOUT WHEN YOU AND LUCIA DISAPPEARED, IF I RECALL.
BUT SOMEONE WAS MISSING, HUH? GUESS WHOSE BODY WAS FOUND STUFFED BETWEEN THE WALLS OF A BUILDING ONE BLOCK AWAY?
OR DID YOU GUESS ALREADY? DID YOU SEE THE NEWS REPORTS WE LEAKED OUT TO TRY AND DRAW YOU AND YOUR SISTER BACK HERE?
TELL ME WHY IT REQUIRED DENTAL RECORDS TO IDENTIFY HARRY BELLINGER, MARIA?
TELL ME -- HOW DID YOUR MOTHER'S OLD BOYFRIEND HAPPEN TO GET HIS FACE RIPPED OFF?!
NYPD
NYPD

SHUT UP!!
YOU DON' KNOW NUTHIN' ABOUT NUTHIN', JOSE! YOU DON' KNOW WHAT HE DID!
YOU EVER STOP TO LOOK PAST THAT STUPID BADGE YOU WEAR--
-- THE MESSED-UP LAWS YOU GET PAID TO UPHOLD--
SHAKK
--AN' THINK TO YOURSELF, THAT MAYBE SOME PEOPLE DESERVE TO GET KILLED?!
MAYBE SOME PEOPLE DO, MARIA...
AFTER THE FACT! THAT'S ALL THE COPS WERE EVER GOOD FOR, RIGHT?
AFTER WE GOT OUR TV STOLEN, THEY CAME!
AFTER DADDY HIT MOMMY, THEY SHOWED UP!
AFTER DADDY WAS FOUND DEAD IN AN ALLEY WITH A NEEDLE IN HIS ARM THEN, THEY TOLD US!
TELL ME, JOSÉ... WHERE WERE YOU AN' YOUR STINKIN' SHINY BADGES WHEN ME AN' LUCIA REALLY NEEDED YOU?
...BUT WANTING SOMEONE TO DIE IS A BIG STEP AWAY FROM ACTUALLY COMMITTING MURDER.
MY JOB ISN'T TO POLICE YOUR THOUGHTS-- BUT YOUR ACTIONS.

I HAVE FERAL'S MUTAGENIC SIGNATURE TRACKED, SAM. SHE'S TWO FLOORS ABOVE YOUR POSITION.
WE'RE GOIN' THERE NOW, CABLE.
JUS' TELL ME IF YOU LOSE THE SIGNAL COMIN' FROM HIDALGO, OKAY?
IF SHE KILLS THE PEACE OFFICER, THEN WILL YOU ACCEPT THE FACT THE GIRL NEEDS TO BE TERMINATED, GUTHRIE?
NO, SHATTERSTAR! MARIA'S NOT GOIN' TO KILL JOSE -- NOT YET, ANYWAY.
SHE'S USIN' HIM TO DRAW US UP-- TO SHOW US SOMETHIN'.
AN' WHAT'S THAT, THORNN?
WHAT HAVEN'T YOU TOLD US YET, WOMAN? WE NEED TA KNOW THE WHOLE TRUTH!
NEVER EXPECT A DEN OF THIEVES TO SAFEGUARD YOUR VALUABLES, CANNONBALL...
...NOR A FAMILY OF LIARS TO PROVIDE YOU WITH THE TRUTH!
IT IS BECOMING INCREASINGLY OBVIOUS THAT THE WORDS WE NEED TO HEAR REGARDING FERAL'S PAST--
--WILL HAVE TO BE RIPPED FROM HER HISSING TONGUE!
KRAKK!

ANY MOVEMENT, DOM?
ZIP.
BE READY. THEY'RE GETTING CLOSER TO HER.
THE ONLY ESCAPE SHE HAS LEFT IS THROUGH THE ROOFTOPS.
FUNNY HOW SHE LET HERSELF GET PINNED LIKE THAT, HUH?
ALMOST AS IF SHE WANTED TO... AS IF SHE HAD A REASON TO.
FERAL IS GOING TO COME OUT INTO THE OPEN-- I'M NOT SURE WHY, BUT MY GUT TELLS ME SHE WILL.
SAY THE WORD WHEN SHE DOES. I HAVE THE SHOT LINED UP ALREADY.
JUST LIKE I HAD... WHEN STRYFE TOOK MY SON, TYLER...
...AND I TOOK THE SHOT ...TO PROTECT THE OTHER MEMBERS OF MY FAMILY...
...I SHOT MY OWN SON...*
NATE--?
THE WORD WON'T BE GIVEN, DOM.
THIS SITUATION IS NOT GOING TO END WITH FERAL'S DEATH!
EVEN IF THAT MEANS...
* SEE CABLE #1-2 --Bob.

"...GIVING HER THE CHANCE TO KILL US--?"
STAY BACK!!
FERAL, STOP IT, GIRL!
YOU AIN'T GETTIN' AWAY FROM HERE, AN' YOU CAN'T KILL ALL OF US!
JUS' GIVE YOURSELF UP, OKAY?
WHAT FOR, SAMMY? SO THAT I CAN GO TO JAIL?
SO I CAN GET LOCKED UP IN A CAGE?
YOU THINK I'M GONNA LET THAT HAPPEN TO ME?!
YOU'RE NOT GETTING OUT OF THIS ONE LIKE YOU DID BEFORE, MARIA.
I WON'T PROTECT YOU AND I WON'T LET YOU RUN AWAY AGAIN!
LET ME RUN AWAY?!
WHAT CHOICE DID YOU EVER GIVE ME, LUCIA?!

I HAD TO LEAVE. AN' YEAH, YOU HELPED ME FIND THE MOR-LOCKS--
--CONVINCED THEM TO TAKE ME IN--
--BUT IF YOU'D DONE WHAT YOU SHOULDA FROM THE BEGINNIN'--
--I NEVER WOULDA BEEN PUT IN THE POSITION I WAS IN!
YOU COVERED UP FOR ME, LUCIA, BUT DON'T EVER THINK YOU PROTECTED ME!
IT'S TENSE IN THERE.
SHE'S SHAKIN' THE COP LIKE A RAG DOLL. HE'S HURTING.
NATE, WE'VE GOT TO DO SOMETHING --!?
LET IT PLAY THROUGH, DOM.
BUT, NATE--!
I SAID LET IT PLAY THROUGH.
OKAY, MARIA! MAYBE YOU'RE RIGHT! I SHOULD'VE DONE MORE--
--I WAS THE OLDER SISTER, BUT I WAS SCARED!!
BUT YOU... YOU NEVER WERE.
WERE YOU--?

SCARED OF WHAT, LUCIA?
OF MOMMA, DRUNK EVERY NIGHT?
OF HARRY TRYIN' TO PAW AT US AFTER SHE PASSED OUT ON THE COUCH?
I WASN'T SCARED ABOUT ANY OF THAT--
--I WAS ANGRY ABOUT IT!!
AN' UNLIKE YOU, BIG SISTER--
--I WAS WILLIN' T'DO SOMETHIN' ABOUT THE PROBLEM!
MOVE IT, JOSE!
FIRE ESCAPE! THEY'RE MOVING OUT!
I'M TRACKING THEM, NATE.
SHE SHOT OUTTA HERE LIKE GREASED SPIT!
THEY'RE HEADING HIGHER, SAM!
SIRYN IS CIRCLING ABOVE NOW!
I GET THE FEELIN' THAT THIS IS ALL COMIN' TO A HEAD--

"--UP ON THE ROOF!"
SKRASHK!
KNOW WHERE WE ARE, HIDAGGY?
REMEMBER THE PIGEON COOP I HAD?
'MEMBER HOW ALLA YOU MADE FUN OF ME--
--FOR WANTIN' TO TAKE CARE OF THE STUPID, SMELLY, DIRTY PIGEONS?
FERAL, STOP THIS MADNESS-- NOW!
KEEP BACK, CASSIDY!
I NEVER HAD NO PROBLEM WITH YOU...
...DON'T MAKE ME HURT YOU NOW.
THE PIGEONS ...?
I REMEMBER THEM, MARIA...
YEAH, I DO!!
THEY WAS ALL I EVER REALLY HAD, JOSE! ALL I EVER NEEDED!
...BUT DO YOU REMEMBER WHAT HAPPENED TO THEM?
THOSE BIRDS WAS THE ONLY THINGS THAT EVER NEEDED ME!!

YOU'RE WRONG, FERAL. *WE* NEEDED YOU.
DURING BATTLES, YOU WATCHED OUR BACKS AN' WE WATCHED YOURS.
AN' YOU NEEDED US, TOO. FOR *FRIENDSHIP*-- FOR A PLACE TO BELONG.
NO! NONE OF YOU EVER WANTED ME AROUND!
NEVER.
STOP *LYING*, MARIA-- TO US-- BUT MOST OF ALL, TO *YOURSELF!*

ME, LYIN'?

THAT'S A LAUGH AN' A HALF, HUH?

GO ON, THEN, LUCIA-- TELL 'EM ALL THE *TRUTH!*

THIS IS THE PLACE TO DO IT, HUH?

IT SURE IS, NIÑA.

OUR POPPA RAN AWAY AFTER CAROLINA WAS BORN.

FOUR KIDS AND NO JOB WAS TOO MUCH FOR HIM.

IT WAS HARD ON US. HARD ON ALL OF US.

MOMMA SAID IT WAS ALL OUR FAULT. ESPECIALLY CAROLINA.

ONE KID TOO MANY, SHE SAID. DROVE POPPA AWAY.

I WAS OLD ENOUGH TO KNOW BETTER, BUT MARIA WAS ONLY SIX...

...SHE HEARD WHAT MOMMA SAID...

...AN' SHE THOUGHT IT WAS CAROLINA'S FAULT-- MAYBE EVEN MATTEO-- BOTH THEIR FAULTS THAT OUR FATHER HAD LEFT US.

OH, LORD.

D-DID FERAL *KILL* YOUR SISTER?

I--I DON'T KNOW--
--I SHOULD HAVE BEEN THERE--WATCHING HER.
IT WAS AS MUCH MY FAULT SHE FELL DOWN THE STAIRS AS ANYONE ELSE'S.
THAT'S RIGHT! THE LITTLE BRAT WENT OVER TO THE STAIRS AN' FELL!
I WAS TRYIN' TO WATCH BOTH MATTEO AN' CAROLINA--'CAUSE YOU WANTED TO GO SEE HIDAGGY OUTSIDE AN' FLIRT WITH HIM, RIGHT?!
IT WASN'T MY FAULT SHE DIED!!
MAYBE NOT, MARIA. BUT I REMEMBER WHEN CAROLINA SHOUTED, WE ALL CAME RUNNING INSIDE--
--WE SAW YOU STANDING AT THE TOP OF THE STAIRS--
--AND MAYBE CAROLINA'S DEATH WAS AN ACCIDENT--
--MAYBE IT WASN'T YOUR FAULT--
--BUT IT WAS STILL A TRAGEDY, MARIA, RIGHT? SO ANSWER ME THEN--
--WHY DO I REMEMBER... YOU LOOKING DOWN AND SMILING?

WHAT ABOUT YOUR BROTHER, FERAL?
WHAT HAPPENED TO HIM?
"HE WAS CHASIN' AFTER MY BIRDS--RUNNIN' ALL OVER THE ROOF."
"DID YOU KILL HIM FOR THAT, FERAL? 'CAUSE HE MESSED WITH YOUR PIGEONS?"
no...
HE TRIPPED OFF THE LEDGE. HE WAS HANGIN' BY HIS FINGERS.
BUT MATTEO WAS ALWAYS WEAK.
HE COULDN'T HANG ON FOR LONG.
HOW LONG DID HE HANG ON FOR, FERAL?
I DON'T KNOW... I DIDN'T COUNT. NOT MY FAULT HE COULDN'T PULL HIMSELF UP, RIGHT?
NOTHIN'S EVER YOUR FAULT, IS IT, GIRL?
WHAT ABOUT YOUR MOMMA'S BOYFRIEND?
TELL 'EM ALL ABOUT HARRY, LUCIA.

HARRY BELLINGER WAS... A PIG.
A COKEHEAD... A DRUNK... HE GOT MOMMA MESSED UP ON DRUGS.
HE WAS ALWAYS TRYING TO... GET AT... ME.
AS I WAS GETTING OLDER, MY MUTATIONS STARTED, REAL SLOW. MUCH SLOWER THAN MARIA'S.
AN' HARRY... HE SAID HE DUG FURRY CHICKS.
"MOMMA WAS PASSED OUT ONE NIGHT-- I WAS SEVENTEEN-- I LEFT-- I WANTED TO GET OUT-- HARRY... HE FOLLOWED ME-- DRAGGED ME INTO AN ALLEY-- I KNEW SAYIN' 'NO' WOULDN'T WORK THIS TIME--
"--THEN WE HEARD... A GROWL... AN ANIMAL SPITTING OUT HATE-- AND WE LOOKED UP--!"
THAT NIGHT, I LOST MY SISTER. AND FERAL HAD TAKEN HER PLACE.
BUT YOU BOTH HID HARRY'S BODY IN AN ABANDONED BUILDING.
AND IT STAYED THERE UNTIL IT WAS FOUND A FEW WEEKS AGO, RIGHT?
THAT'S WHY YOU CAME BACK, FERAL?
'CAUSE WHEN YOU SAW THE NEWS REPORTS ABOUT HARRY, YOU KNEW THE TRUTH WOULD GET OUT?
YEAH, SAMMY, YOU'RE SO SMART FOR AN IN-BRED MOUNTAIN MAN, HUH?
I GOT THE TIP THAT THE FRIENDS OF HUMANITY WAS GONNA SPRING LUCIA, BRING HER HERE AN' MAKE HER PAY FOR "HER" CRIMES--
--BUT THAT WAS ALL JUST A SET UP SO YOU COULD TRAP ME!

THORNN CAN'T GO T' JAIL FOR CRIMES YOU
CRIMES?
CAROLINA WAS AN ACCIDENT? WHO KNOWS?
MATTEO, TOO? MAYBE.
WITH HARRY BELLINGER, MAYBE YOU COULD MAKE A CASE FOR SELF-DEFENSE; AH AIN'T NO LAWYER...
...BUT WHAT ABOUT YOUR MOTHER, FERAL? WHAT HAPPENED T' HER?
THE PIGEONS.
AFTER WE GOT RID OF HARRY, SHE WAS MAD...
...SO TO GET BACK AT ME, SHE KILLED THE PIGEONS!!
I HATED HER.
SO YOU WANNA KNOW WHAT I DID, SAMMY?
I KILLED HER.

--JUST LIKE I'M GONNA KILL ALLA YOU!!
NO, GIRL...
...THERE'S BEEN MORE'N ENOUGH DYIN' DONE HERE.
TOO MUCH PAIN, TOO MUCH BLOOD.
WE CAME HERE TONIGHT T' END IT!
AN' NOW THAT WE'VE FOUND OUT THE WHOLE TRUTH-- END IT, WE WILL!!
SHWAFOOM
YOU CAN COME UP WITH ALL THE EXCUSES YOU WANT TO, FERAL--
--BUT THE BOTTOM LINE AIN'T THAT YOU KILLED THE PEOPLE YOU DID BECAUSE YOU HATED THEM, OR 'CAUSE THEY HATED YOU--
--YOU DID IT BECAUSE YOU'VE ALWAYS HATED YOURSELF!
AN' THERE'S TOO MUCH HATE IN THIS WORLD TO LET SOMEONE LIKE YOU KEEP SPREADIN' IT AROUND EVERYWHERE YOU GO!
WHICH LEAVES YOU ONLY ONE PLACE LEFT TO GO. THE PLACE YOU SHOULDA BEEN AT A LONG, LONG TIME AGO.. DETECTIVE--?
MARIA CALLASANTOS-- YOU'RE UNDER ARREST FOR THE MURDERS OF--

SPECIAL REPORT
--CAROLINA, MATTEO AND MARCELLA CALLASANTOS, AS WELL AS A MAN NAMED HARRY BELLINGER--
THE YOUNG MUTANT WOMAN CHARGED IS ALSO A MEMBER OF THE TERRORIST MUTANT LIBERATION FRONT--
3 LIVE
MUTANTS BUSTED
--AND USED THE MLF TO KIDNAP HER SISTER AND NYPD DETECTIVE JOSE HIDALGO FROM THEIR TRANS-PORT TO RYKER'S ISLAND.
THE HEROIC HIDALGO AND LUCIA CALLASANTOS, THE SISTER TRAPPED BY THIS TRAGEDY, WERE ABLE TO FEND OFF THEIR MLF KIDNAPERS--
--AND APPREHEND FERAL.
DOC
DOC
CNN
IT IS EXPECTED THAT LUCIA WILL NOT BE INDICTED FOR HER ROLE IN COVERING UP HER SISTER'S ACTIONS--
--BUT THAT FERAL WILL BE INDICTED ON AT LEAST ONE MURDER CHARGE...
NO EASY SOLUTIONS, HUH?
Hugo's Electronic
BEARS
97
IT WASN'T AN EASY PROBLEM, SAM.
BUT BLAMIN' THE MLF FOR WHAT HAPPENED? THAT WAS A NEAT TRICK.
I CAN'T TAKE ALL THE CREDIT THERE. THE IDEA CAME FROM THE YOUNG WOMAN WHO TIPPED ME OFF WHEN FERAL FIRST ARRIVED IN MANHATTAN.

SHE ALSO HAPPENED TO FEED FERAL THE FALSE INFORMATION WHICH BROUGHT HER TO THE BRONX.
BUT WHO WOULD BENEFIT FROM HELPIN' US OUT, MAKIN' THE MLF LOOK BAD AN' GETTIN' RID OF FERAL ALL AT
THE
SAME
TIME--?
DANI MOONSTAR ?!?
SAM. CABLE. THINGS WORKED OUT JUST FINE, DIDN'T THEY?
BUT YOU'RE WITH THE MLF NOW--AREN'T YOU?--WHY WOULD YOU HELP US?!
MAYBE BECAUSE, SAM, LIKE YOU, I ALWAYS *HAVE* BEEN--
--AND *STILL* AM--
--SOMEONE WHO CARES ABOUT THE *TRUTH*...
...AND ABOUT *FAMILY*.
End

MARVEL COMICS
JAN 42
X-MEN
X-FORCE
APPROVED BY THE COMICS CODE AUTHORITY
TONY DANIEL -W- KEVIN CONRAD '94

STAN LEE PRESENTS
THE UNLIKELIEST OF FIRST MEETINGS BETWEEN X-FORCE AND GENERATION X!
SO, WHAT WERE YOU FEELING, JAMES?
WHAT DO YOU MEAN?
MY BROTHER WAS DEAD!
I WAS WATCHING HIS BODY BURNING IN FRONT OF MY EYES--
--I COULD PRACTICALLY SEE HIS SPIRIT RISING FROM THE FLAMES--
--WHAT DO YOU THINK I WAS FEELING?!
I DON'T KNOW. I'D RATHER YOU TELL ME.

YOU'RE THE TELE-PATH, AREN'T YOU?
EMMA FROST, THE COLD AND CALCULATING WHITE QUEEN?
YOU'RE THE ONE TAKING A MENTAL STROLL THROUGH MY MEMORIES--
--SO YOU MUST HAVE IT ALL FIGURED OUT ALREADY, RIGHT?
I HAVE. WE ARE WITNESSIN THE MOMENT TH BOY NAMED JAMES PROUDSTAR
--BECAME A MAN.
BUT THE ROAD YOU CHOSE-- THE PATH OF WAR, IF I MAY BE SO TRITE--
--WAS NEVER REALLY TRUE TO YOUR SPIRIT, WAS IT, JAMES?
I WAS ANGRY.
I LOST MY BROTHER BE-FORE I EVER REALLY GOT A CHANCE TO KNOW HIM.
I BLAMED CHARLES XAVIER FOR THAT. BECAUSE HE TOOK JOHN AWAY.
MADE HIM AN X-MAN. AND THAT GOT HIM KILLED.
I WAS WRONG, THOUGH.
NO ONE GOT JOHNN KILLED BUT JOHNNY.
AND YOU WERE EQUALLY WRONG TO BLAME THE HELL-FIRE CLUB--
--FOR THE DESTRUCTION OF YOUR RESERVA-TION AND ITS PEOPLE.

YOU SEEM TO HAVE QUITE A PENCHANT FOR DOING THAT, DON'T YOU?
DOING WHAT?
BLAMING THE WRONG PEOPLE FOR TRAGEDIES IN YOUR LIFE.
MISPLACING YOUR EMOTIONAL BAGGAGE.
YOU SHOULD TALK, LADY.
LOOK AT YOU NOW. TRYING ALL OVER AGAIN WITH A NEW GROUP OF KIDS.
WHY? THE HELLIONS ARE DEAD--
--AND THIS GENERATION X CAN NEVER BE THEM.
NOW, JAMES, YOU DIDN'T COME TO MASSACHUSETTS WITH YOUR X-FORCE FRIENDS IN ORDER TO TALK ABOUT ME, DID YOU?
SO LET'S TALK ABOUT YOU THEN. AND WHY YOU CONTINUE TO LIVE A LIFE THAT BRINGS YOU SO LITTLE HAPPINESS...
...THERESA, TELL ME ABOUT THIS LAD, JIMMY.
HE SEEMS T'CARE FOR YOU QUITE A BIT.

HE'S A GOOD MAN, DA.
HE HELPED ME THROUGH SOME DIFFICULT TIMES, YE KNOW.
THE DRINKING, THEN, THAT YE TOLD ME ABOUT?
A-AYE. HE WAS THERE FOR ME BEFORE IT BECAME A PERMANENT PROBLEM.
MADE ME SEE I DIDNAE NEED T'USE LIQUOR AS A CRUTCH AGAINST THE THINGS THAT HAUNTED ME.
IT WAS LIKE A LIGHT BEIN' TURNED ON IN ME HEAD, DA--LIGHT'S ON, PROBLEM'S GONE!
DON'T EVER THINK THE SOLUTIONS T'THOSE KINDS OF THINGS ARE EVER SO EASY, LUV.
BUT I AM HAPPY T'SEE YE HAD PEOPLE T'TURN TO.
TELL ME, D'YE LOVE HIM AS MUCH AS HE LOVES YOU?
I--I LOVE HIM, OF COURSE--BUT LIKE A FRIEND--
--THERE'S NOTHING BE-TWEEN US LIKE THAT!

OH--?
OH, WHAT?
I JUST DON'T THINK JIMMY FEELS THE SAME WAY YE DO, 'TIS ALL.
TIS DIFFICULT ENOUGH T'BE IN THE LINE OF WORK WE'RE IN WITHOUT FEELINGS OF UNREQUITED LOVE TOSSIN' ABOUT IN OUR HEARTS.
WELL THEN, SPEAKIN' OF UNREQUITED LOVE--
--TELL ME HOW MOIRA MACTAGGERT FEELS--
--BEIN' AN OCEAN AWAY AT MUIR ISLAND--
--WHILE YE'RE WORKIN' WITH MISS EMMA "DO-YOU-THINK-MY-GARTER BELT-LOOKS-GOOD-WITH-THESE-LACE-STOCKINGS" FROST?
THE TRUTH? IT WAS ENOUGH T'MAKE HER--
SKREEEEEEEM
WHY DO YOU CONTINUE TO STAY WITH X-FORCE, JAMES?

THEY NEED ME.
THERE IS LITTLE THAT YOUR ENHANCED STRENGTH BRINGS TO X-FORCE THAT OTHERS CAN'T DUPLICATE OR SURPASS IN OTHER WAYS.
FOR WHAT?
AND WHAT OF YOUR ESPOUSED "CAUSE" UNDER CABLE'S GUIDANCE?
"DO UNTO THEM BEFORE THEY DO UNTO YOU"--?
HOW CHILDISHLY USELESS AN APPROACH TO LIFE.
WELL, IT SOUNDED PRETTY GOOD WHEN WE FIRST STARTED OUT.
WEREN'T ANGER AND REVENGE YOUR STATED MOTIVATIONS FOR JOINING THEM?
DO YOU REMEMBER HOW IT FELT, JAMES--
--AFTER YOU FOUND THE CAMP VERDE APACHE RESER-VATION DECIMATED--
--AND ALL OF YOUR PEOPLE--
--YOUR FAMILY AND FRIENDS--DEAD--?!

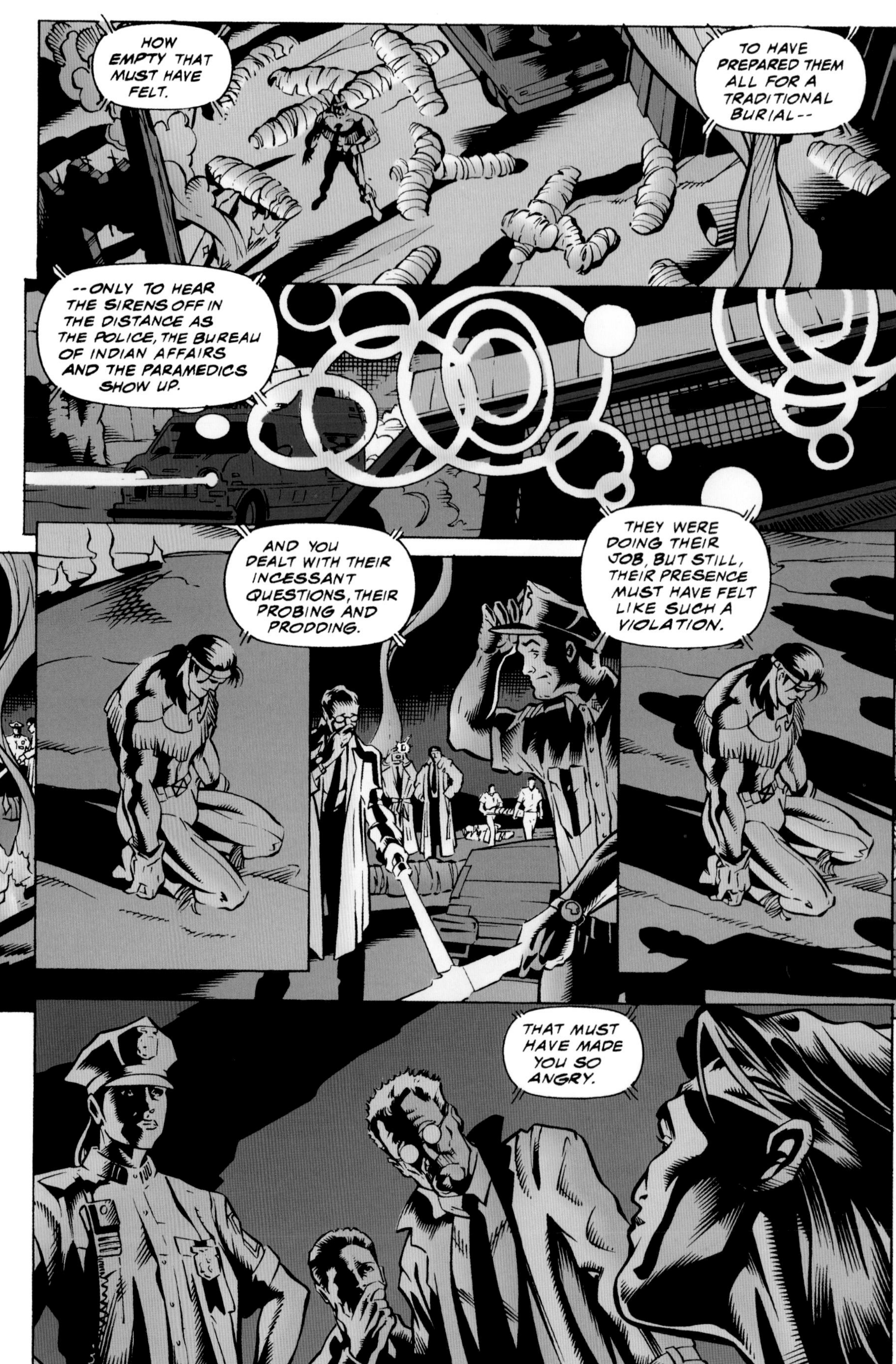
HOW EMPTY THAT MUST HAVE FELT.
TO HAVE PREPARED THEM ALL FOR A TRADITIONAL BURIAL--
--ONLY TO HEAR THE SIRENS OFF IN THE DISTANCE AS THE POLICE, THE BUREAU OF INDIAN AFFAIRS AND THE PARAMEDICS SHOW UP.
AND YOU DEALT WITH THEIR INCESSANT QUESTIONS, THEIR PROBING AND PRODDING.
THEY WERE DOING THEIR JOB, BUT STILL, THEIR PRESENCE MUST HAVE FELT LIKE SUCH A VIOLATION.
THAT MUST HAVE MADE YOU SO ANGRY.

THE MASSACRE WAS THE WORK OF PROFESSIONALS, THEY DETERMINED.
A CLINICAL, METHODICAL, MILITARY-STYLE SANCTIONING OF AN ENTIRE TOWN-FULL OF PEOPLE.

HOW DID THAT MAKE YOU FEEL?

ANGRY.

FURIOUS!

I THOUGHT THE HELLFIRE CLUB HAD SLAUGHTERED EVERYONE I EVER CARED ABOUT JUST BECAUSE I HAD DECIDED TO LEAVE THE HELLIONS!

YOU WERE THINKING NO SUCH THING AND YOU KNOW IT!!

YOU KNOW-- YOU HAVE ALWAYS KNOWN-- IN YOUR HEART--

--THAT THE HELLFIRE CLUB NEVER HAD ANYTHING TO DO WITH THE MURDER OF YOUR PEOPLE!

SMAKT

WHY WOULD I HAVE WANTED VENGEANCE ON YOU FOR LEAVING US?
WHO WAS IT THAT *ENCOURAGED* YOU TO GO BACK HOME AGAIN?

YOU DID.

AND DO YOU REMEMBER *WHY* I DID SO?

BECAUSE AFTER THE INCIDENT WITH XAVIER, WHEN I LEARNED I WAS *WRONG* TO HAVE BLAMED HIM FOR JOHNNY'S DEATH--

--YOU KNEW I WASN'T HAPPY-- THAT I HAD LOST A SENSE OF PLACE AND A REASON FOR EVEN *BEING* HERE AT ALL ANYMORE.

YOU CAME TO US SO I COULD HELP YOU BECOME LIKE YOUR *BROTHER*--

--AND THEN LEARNED THAT WAS NO LONGER WHAT YOU WANTED OUT OF LIFE.

SO TELL ME THEN, JAMES, WHY DO YOU *PERSIST* IN FOLLOWING IN *JOHN PROUDSTAR'S* FOOTSTEPS?

YOU SURE DO GOT A FUNNY WAY OF FOLLOWIN' YOUR BIG BROTHER'S LEAD, GIRL.
AH MEAN, LOOKIN' TA PRO-FESSOR XAVIER TA HELP YOU LEARN TA USE YOUR MUTANT POWERS IS ALL WELL AN' GOOD. IT WORKED FOR ME.
AN' THE MASS. ACAD. HERE HAS THE WESTCHESTER MANSION BEAT TA ALL GET OUT--
-- BUT REALLY, PAIGE -- THE WHITE QUEEN IS YOUR TEACHER ?!
NO.
MORE LIKE THE PRINCIPAL, SAM.
WHAT KINDUVA ROLE MODEL DOES SHE MAKE, GIRL ?
AH MEAN, SHORTA THE FACT SHE'S FOUGHT THE X-MEN MORE TIMES THAN FINGERS AH GOT TA COUNT--
-- SHE ALSO GOT HER LAST GROUP OF STUDENTS KILLED!
MOMMA ASKED ME TO CHECK ON YOU, PAIGE. TA MAKE SURE YOU'RE OKAY UP IN "YANKEELAND" AS SHE CALLED IT.
NEVER MIND YOU'RE IN RED SOX TERRITORY, BUT AH FIGURED--

THAT YOU'D COME UP HERE AN' LECTURE ME?
YOU KNOW HOW AH-- HOW I-- LOOOVE TO HEAR--
-- FROM THE SAM GUTHRIE BOOK ON "HOW TO BE A RIGHT PROPER MUTANT"--!
OH, NOW AH'M BLEEDIN'. YOU CUT DEEP, GIRL.
AH'M NOT TRYIN' TA TELL YOU HOW YOU SHOULD--
"LIVE YOAH LIFE, PAIGE, BUT WHEN AH WAS WITH THE NEW MUTANTS
WE WOULD RUN OFF BEHIND THE PROFESSOR'S BACK THEAH
THEN WE'D GET MAGNETO TA FOLD OUR LAUNDRY
AN' WE'D ZIP ON UP TA ASGARD WITH BIRD BRAIN SQUAKKIN' IN OUR EARS.
HA-YUCK! HA-YUCK!
AH NEVER SAID HA-YUCK.
YOU'RE MY LITTLE SISTER, PAIGE.
YOU CAN AT LEAST PRETEND TA RESPECT ME.
I DO RESPECT YOU, SAM--IT'S JUST SOMETIMES I DON'T UNDERSTAND YOU.
YESSIREEE, GOYS AND BIRLS
NOT SINCE BILL BUCKNER LET THAT BASEBALL ROLL BETWEEN HIS LEGS
HAS BOSTON SEEN SUCH A POTENTIAL TRAGEDY IN THE MAKING!!

IN THIS CORNER, WEIGHING NINETY-FIVE-- IF SHE'S A POUND--

-- WITH GOLDEN LOCKS WE ALL KNOW ARE BORN OF NATURE'S FINEST CHEMICALS, IS BOOMER, QUEEN OF CONSUMPTION!

CHALLENGING HER PEROXIDE SPENDING MIGHT IS THE HOBBIT FROM HOLLYWOOD

THE PIPSQUEAK FROM THE PACIFIC

THE PRINCESS OF PURCHASE HERSELF-- JUBILEE!

A NO-HOLDS BARRED, THREE-HOUR SHOPPING SPREE AT FANUEIL HALL!

WHOEVER SPENDS THE MOST OF CABLE'S OR IRISH'S MONEY IS THE HEAVYWEIGHT CHAMPION MALL RAT OF THE WORLD!!

YOU COWPOKES WANNA SEE THE AMERICAN ECONOMY RECOVER BY DINNERTIME?

GUESS NOT!

YOU KNOW YOU'RE WRONG--

HAH
HA
HAH
AIN'T WE A PAIR, HUH?
THE WAY I FIGURE, BIG BROTHER, BEING MUTANTS IS EASY FOR US--

"--NOW BEING FAMILY, THAT'S HARD!!"
HAVE FUN, KIDS.
THE WAY THEY'RE MOVING, YE'D THINK THEY'D GOTTEN HOLD OF EMMA'S PLATINUM CARD.
OR SOMEONE'S.
BECAUSE EMMA, THEY ARE-- I GUESS.
WHAT IS IT THEY DO THAT HAS ANYTHING TO DO WITH WHAT YOU WANT?
WHAT DO ANY OF US WANT?
A PLACE TO FEEL COMFORTABLE?
PEOPLE WHO YOU LIKE AND LIKE YOU BACK?
A REASON TO GET OUT OF BED IN THE MORNING?
WHY IS IT THAT YOU THINK OF THEM ALL AS YOUR FAMILY NOW?
ALL LOGICAL DESIRES... WERE YOU A NORMAL YOUNG MAN.
BUT WHAT NINETEEN YEAR OLD WITH A CHOICE--
--WOULD LIVE UNDERGROUND WITH A GROUP OF OUTLAWS--
--WORKING FOR A MAN WHO BELIEVES THAT IN ORDER TO PREVENT ANARCHY, ONE MUST FOMENT CHAOS?

WELL, WHAT AM I SUPPOSED TO DO?
KRUNCHK
YOU TELL ME!
WHAT HAS MY LIFE-- OR THE PEOPLE WHO TAUGHT ME, INCLUDING YOU-- EVER DONE TO PRE-PARE ME FOR ANYTHING EXCEPT WHAT I'M DOING NOW?
JAMES, STOP YOUR WHINING-- PLEASE.
I'M SO TIRED OF PEOPLE BLAMING OTHERS FOR THEIR MISFOR-TUNES. IT'S SO TRENDY.
DO YOU UNDERSTAND WHAT I'M SAYING?
WHAT YOU ARE TODAY IS, OF COURSE, A DIRECT RESULT OF THE IN-FLUENCES YOU'VE EXPERIENCED--
--AND THE HARDSHIPS YOU ENDURED AS A CHILD--
-- BUT WHAT YOU WILL DEVELOP INTO AS A YOUNG ADULT SHOULD BE A CONSCIOUS AND DIRECT CHOICE ON YOUR PART.
I THINK I HEARD ALL THIS ON OPRAH LAST WEEK.
YOU SURVIVED, JAMES! OF ALL MY ORIGINAL CLASS OF HELLIONS, ONLY YOU AND MANUEL MANAGED TO DO THAT!
DO YOU REALIZE HOW VALUABLE THE GIFT OF LIFE REALLY IS?
I NEVER APPRECIATED IT MYSELF... UNTIL JUST RECENTLY...
...IT INFURIATES ME TO SEE YOU DOING SO LITTLE WITH THE OPPORTUNITIES AVAILABLE TO YOU!

WHICH BEGGARS THE QUESTION...
... WHAT IS IT THAT YOU WANT TO BE, JAMES PROUDSTAR?
I DON'T KNOW.
AND HOW EXACTLY WILL YOU EVER LEARN WHAT IT IS IF YOU PERSIST IN PERPETUATING THE SAME MISTAKES WHICH HAVE MADE YOU SO UNHAPPY TO BEGIN WITH?
I... DON'T KNOW...
SO WE COME BACK ONCE AGAIN TO WHAT I ASKED OF YOU EARLIER...
... GIVE ME ONE GOOD REASON WHY YOU'RE STAYING WITH X-FORCE?

INTERLUDE

MRRRRRRRRAAAAAAAAAAAAAA

AT THE MAIN RESEARCH FACILITIES FOR THE VERSCHLAGEN BIOCHEMICAL RESEARCH ORGANIZATION IN NEUSTRELITZ, GERMANY...

...AN APPARENT INCIDENCE OF INDUSTRIAL ESPIONAGE TURNS UGLY...

ARTOFFELKOPF

SHUFF

SHUFF

HALT!

GESTORBEN?
JA.

< SHOW ME HIS FACE. >

-GASP-
< WE DID NOT KNOW, FRAU VERSCHLAGEN! >
< HE TURNED TO FIRE UPON US --
-- WE MERELY DEFENDED OURSELVES! >

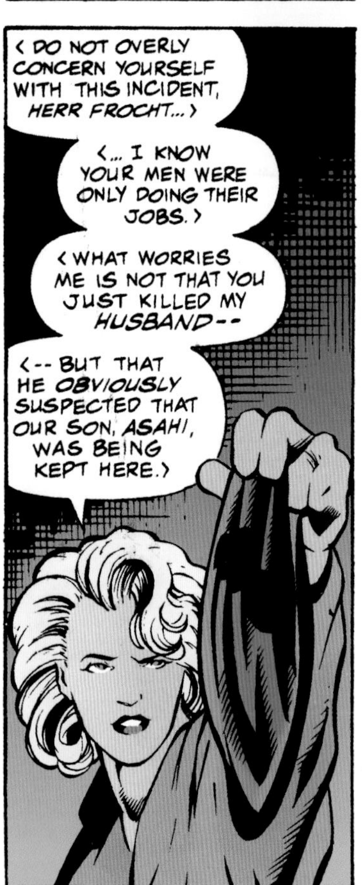
< DO NOT OVERLY CONCERN YOURSELF WITH THIS INCIDENT, HERR FROCHT... >
< ... I KNOW YOUR MEN WERE ONLY DOING THEIR JOBS. >
< WHAT WORRIES ME IS NOT THAT YOU JUST KILLED MY HUSBAND --
< -- BUT THAT HE OBVIOUSLY SUSPECTED THAT OUR SON, ASAHI, WAS BEING KEPT HERE. >

< IT STANDS TO REASON THEN, THAT HIS EMPLOYERS SUSPECT AS WELL. >

< WHICH MEANS WE HAD BEST PREPARE FOR A LITTLE VISIT FROM THE JAPANESE CLAN YASHIDA! >

XAVIER'S...
WHAT KIND OF A QUESTION IS THAT, EMMA?
A VALID ONE, I THINK, IN LIGHT OF EVERYTHING WE'VE DISCUSSED TODAY.
"WHY DO I STAY WITH X-FORCE?" BECAUSE THEY'RE MY FRIENDS, THAT'S WHY.
THEY'RE WILLING TO FIGHT FOR SOMETHING IMPORTANT. SOMETHING I BELIEVE IN.
AND THAT IS?
PEACE.
AH, I SEE. ANYTHING ELSE?
WELL... THERESA CASSIDY. SHE NEEDS ME.

DOES SHE REALLY?

YEAH--SHE'S HAD A HARD LIFE--SHE'S NEEDED A SHOULDER TO CRY ON--
--SOMEONE SHE CAN DE-PEND ON. I'VE BEEN THERE FOR HER.
SHE HAD A BIT OF A... PROBLEM... THAT I HELPED HER OUT WITH.

WE WENT TO IRELAND TOGETHER.
AND JUST LAST WEEK SHE HAD A SITUATION WITH HER UNCLE AND DEADPOOL WHICH WE TALKED ABOUT.
SHE STILL NEEDS ME. I'M NOT ABOUT TO LET HER DOWN.

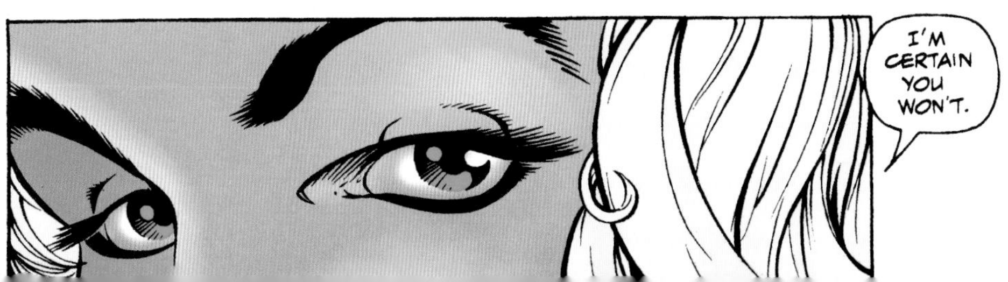
I'M CERTAIN YOU WON'T.

WHAT WERE YOU FEELING WHEN YOU WATCHED YOUR BROTHER'S BODY BURNING IN FRONT OF YOUR EYES, JAMES?
WHAT WERE YOU REALLY FEELING AS YOU FOUND YOUR FAMILY DEAD?
DO YOU KNOW WHAT I THINK?
NO... BUT I'M SURE YOU'RE GOING TO TELL ME.
I THINK THAT YOU'RE AFRAID TO CONFRONT WHAT YOU REALLY FELT.
BECAUSE IF YOU DO, IT MIGHT FORCE YOU TO FINALLY SEVER THE TIES YOU REFUSE TO LET GO OF.
TIES WHICH BIND YOU TO A PAST WHICH HAS NOTHING TO DO WITH WHAT IS REALLY INSIDE YOU.
WHICH KEEP YOU FROM BECOMING WHAT YOU MIGHT OTHERWISE WANT TO.
YEAH... FOOTBALL HERO, MARRIED, THE HOUSE WITH A WHITE PICKET FENCE AND TWO KIDS.
RIGHT.
YOU KNOW SO MUCH, EMMA, THEN TELL ME HOW YOU FELT...
...WHEN YOU FIRST FOUND OUT THAT THE HELLIONS HAD ALL BEEN KILLED.

I WAS... MAD AT THEM.
FOR NOT HAVING BEEN BETTER.
FOR HAVING BEEN UNDONE BY THE VERY FORCES THEY WERE TRAINED TO FIGHT AGAINST.

BULL! YOU KNOW WHAT I THINK, EMMA-- I THINK THIS IS ALL A JOKE!
SURROUNDING YOURSELF WITH A BUNCH OF KIDS ALL OVER AGAIN--
--LIKE YOU'LL MAKE A DIFFERENCE THIS TIME!
YOU'RE JUST USING THEM--
--LIKE MAYBE IF THEY'RE HERE, YOU'LL FORGET THAT DEEP DOWN INSIDE, YOU KNOW YOU'RE A FAILURE--
--AND THAT YOUR FAILURE RESULTED IN THE DEATHS OF SIX PEOPLE!
SLAM!

CRASH!

AFRAID.
YOU WERE TERRIFIED, JAMES.

HEY, GUYS.
HOW'D THINGS GO WITH MS. FROST?

S'WELL AS CAN BE EXPECTED, I GUESS.
I'M BACK TO SQUARE ONE REGARDING WHO REALLY DID DESTROY CAMP VERDE TWO YEARS AGO--
--BUT AT LEAST I KNOW IT WASN'T THE HELLFIRE CLUB.
WHAT WERE YE UP THERE ALL AFTER-NOON CHATTIN' ABOUT THEN?

NOTHING MUCH.
SCARED TO DEATH. SCARED OF LIFE.

AND YOU STILL ARE. TERRIFIED. KNOWING THAT COULD HAVE BEEN YOU.
EVERY DAY SPENT FIGHTING THIS UGLY WAR COULD BE YOUR LAST.
AND YOU GET BY, CON-VINCED THAT YOU'RE JUST A HEARTBEAT AWAY FROM LOVE AND LIFE.

WHEN THE SAD REALITY YOU REFUSE TO ADMIT--
-- IS THAT YOU'RE MUCH CLOSER TO BEING A SIMPLE HEARTBEAT AWAY...
...FROM MISERY AND DEATH.

ALL THAT TIME AN' "NOTHING MUCH" IS THE ANSWER?
YOU KNOW EMMA... STUBBORN TO THE MAX.
SHE IGNORED EVERYTHING I HAD TO SAY.

GREAT TIMIN', GANG!
WE'RE GOING INTO THE CITY TO CATCH UP WITH THE OTHERS.
WANNA JOIN US AND MAKE A PARTY OUT OF IT?

YEAH, PAIGE...

...A PARTY SOUNDS LIKE A GREAT IDEA.
UHM... WHAT'RE WE ALL CELEBRATIN'? THEN, JIMMY?
HOW ABOUT--TO TOMORROW?
THAT'LL DO FOR STARTERS...

A LIE OF THE MIND

FABIAN NICIEZA · TERRY DODSON · KEVIN CONRAD
WRITER · GUEST PENCILER · INKER

PAT BROSSEAU & CHRIS ELIOPOULOS - LETTERS MARIE JAVINS - COLOR ART

BOB HARRAS - EDITOR TOM DEFALCO - EDITOR IN CHIEF

MARVEL COMICS
FEB • 43
X-MEN
X-FORCE
APPROVED BY THE COMICS CODE AUTHORITY
TONY DANIEL
KEVIN CONRAD

THE FIRST WORDS SAM GUTHRIE REMEMBERS ROBERTO DACOSTA EVER SAYING TO HIM WERE NOT KIND ONES.
FROM THIS VERY UNCOMFORTABLE BEGINNING, EVEN-TUALLY, A WONDERFUL FRIENDSHIP WAS FORGED.
THROUGH GOOD TIMES AND BAD, WITH THE NEW MUTANTS AND THEN X-FORCE--
--THEY CAME TO DEPEND ON EACH OTHER FOR SO MANY LITTLE THINGS.
NOW BOBBY NEEDS SAM TO DO ONE SIMPLE, YET NEARLY IM-POSSIBLE, FAVOR--TO FIND HIM--TO SAVE HIM--AND BRING HIM HOME.
BUT SAM HAS FAILED HIS BEST FRIEND TIME AND AGAIN.

STAN LEE PRESENTS A SHOCKING TURNING POINT FOR X-FORCE!
TEAPOT IN A TEMPEST
FABIAN NICIEZA WRITER TONY DANIEL PENCILER KEVIN CONRAD INKER
CHRIS ELIOPOULOS JUST MARRIED MIKE THOMAS JUST COLORING BOB HARRAS JUST HARRASSING
THE MUTANT LIBERATION FRONT HAD KIDNAPPED NATIONAL SECURITY ADVISOR HENRY PETER GYRICH.
X-FORCE MOUNTED A RESCUE ATTEMPT.
THEY SUCCEEDED IN SAVING THE LIFE OF A MAN WHO HATES THEIR VERY EXISTENCE, BUT LOST TWO OF THEIR OWN IN THE PROCESS.
FERAL DEFECTED TO THE MLF.
SUNSPOT DISAP-PEARED WHEN HIS POWERS MYSTERIOUSLY INTERFACED WITH THE MUTANT TELEPORTER NAMED LOCUS.
HE HAS BEEN MISSING EVER SINCE.
AFTER MONTHS OF LOOKING FOR THIS FRUSTRATING NEEDLE IN A HAYSTACK, SAM HAS BECOME DOWN-RIGHT DESPERATE...

ANY LUCK FINDING 'BERTO?
HAVEN'T TURNED ON THE MODIFIED CEREBRO UNIT YET.
YE THINK RUNNIN' PROFESSOR XAVIER'S MUTANT-DETECTION SYSTEM THROUGH CABLE'S TIME-DISPLACEMENT CORE IS GOING T'WORK, SAM?
AH'M TOSSIN' A PRAYER TO THE WIND, TERRY, AH KNOW.
LORD, PLEASE LET THIS WORK.
COMPUTER: END HOLO-RETRIEVAL PROGRAM.
CABLE'S TDC HAS BEEN OUT OF POWER AND LYIN' AT THE BOTTOM OF THE PACIFIC OCEAN FOR MONTHS NOW--
--BUT MAYBE--JUST MAYBE--I CAN ACCESS ITS TEMPORAL SENSORY ARRAY...
MAKE YOU SWE

HHMMMMMMMMM
...USIN' THE TWO IN TANDEM T'CREATE A CROSS-TIME MUTAGENIC ENERGY SIGNATURE SWEEP?
PRETTY AMBITIOUS.
LOCUS COULD TELEPORT ANYWHERE SHE'D BEEN--OR ANYWHERE HER TARGET HAD BEEN.
YEAH. BOTH THE PROFESSOR AND CABLE DOUBTED IT WOULD WORK. BUT SINCE THEY'RE OVER IN ISRAEL, I DECIDED TA GIVE IT A SHOT NOW. *
AH KNOW--AN' WHERE SUNSPOT IS CONCERNED, THAT COULD RANGE FROM ASGARD TO OUTER SPACE TO A DIFFERENT TIME ALTOGETHER!
BUT AH HAVE FAITH HE'S STILL ALIVE. AH HAVE TO.
*SEE CURRENT ISSUES OF X-MEN, UNCANNY AND CABLE. --BOB
MMMMMM
AND WE DO TOO, GUTHRIE, EVEN THOUGH WE HAVEN'T ALWAYS SAID IT.
SO LET'S FIRE UP THAT THERE DOO-HICKEY AND SEE WHAT COOKS!
THANKS, JIMMY.
DIDN'T SEE YOU WALK IN, BUT WHERE SIRYN GOES, WARPATH IS SOON TO FOLLOW, HUH?
WHO CAN KNOCK THE VIEW?
OKAY... HERE GOES...
KLIK
BOOSTER-GAIN ON-LINE:.
TEMPORAL SENSORY ACCESS INITIATED:.
COMMENCING SEARCH:.
SENSORY SCAN COMPLETED:.
THAT WAS A LOT FASTER THAN AH EXPECTED!
TARGET LOCATED:.
SAM, THERE'S A REASON WHY THE SEARCH WAS SO QUICK--BUT I DON'T THINK YOU'RE GOING TO LIKE IT, MUCH--
--DO YOU SEE THAT?! BOBBY'S HERE!!
I MEAN, ON EARTH--RIGHT NOW!
MAY THE LORD HAVE MERCY--
--HAVE A LOOK AT WHERE HE IS.

GREENWICH VILLAGE IN LOWER MANHATTAN...
OKAY, BOOMER, GIRL, YOU'RE THE ONE WHO TOLD THE BOYS YOU WANTED TO BE ON YOUR OWN TONIGHT.
COULDA GONE MOSHIN' WITH RIC AN' SHATTY, BUT NOOO--
--YOU GOTTA START GETTIN' ALL MATURE-LIKE LATELY.
ALL CHINESE CUISINE
Frenchie's VIDEO
TREASURE CHEST
JACOBS 3's LIQUOR
HOTT
GIRLS GIRLS GIRLS
LIVE XXX
JUST... THINGS AREN'T THE SAME ANYMORE AN' YOU KNOW IT, GIRL.
DEALIN' WITH SAMMY-BOY, THE HUNK YOU LOVE BEIN' IMMOR-TAL...
... BOBBY MISSIN', MOONSTAR PLAYIN' BOTH SIDES OF THE FENCE...
... AN' THE JUNK WITH FERAL...
CHILD WATCH
... AN' DOUG RAMSEY KINDASORTANOTREALLY BEIN' ALIVE AGAIN*...
... ALL THAT STUFF GOIN' DOWN HAS MADE TABITHA, THE PEROXIDE FOX, START SEEING HERSELF A LITTLE DIFFERENTLY IS ALL.
LOOK AT THESE STREETS.
THIS COULDA BEEN ME.
* SEE RECENT ISSUES OF EXCALIBUR.--BOB
A RUNAWAY. SEVENTEEN YEARS OLD AND WORKING THE CORNERS.
WHO WOULDA HELPED ME OUT THEN? WHO WOULDA COME TO MY RESCUE?
CALL ME KELLY.
YEAH, SURE.
CW
NIGHT GAMES
WHAT'S YOUR NAME?

WHAT'S THE DIFF?
MAYBE BECAUSE A FRIENDSHIP HAS TO START SOMEWHERE.
IT'S A PLACE TO COME IN... FOR HELP--IF YOU'D LIKE.
JIMMY D. AIN'T GONNA LIKE YOU TALKIN' WITH HER, PRIS!
LEAVE HER ALONE, OKAY?!
FIRST NAMES SEEM LIKE A GOOD BET.
CHILDWATCH ORGANIZATION, HUH? OVER ON BLEECKER, RIGHT?
NO--SHE'S RIGHT--HE WOULD GET MAD.
SORRY-- I--I GOTTA GO--
THE YOUNG GIRL RUNS OFF.
DON'T LISTEN TO THEM-- WAIT--
KELLY HITCHUCK HAS A FEW CHOICE WORDS FOR THE OLDER WORKING WOMEN WHO LAUGHED AT HER--
--AND THEN SHE LEAVES, IN SEARCH OF ANOTHER YOUNG SOUL TO TRY AND SAVE THIS NIGHT.
1-800-555-SA
WE'RE HERE TO H
HMMM. OKAY, BOOMER, YOU WANNA START ACTING LIKE AN ADULT...
...THEN START BY ACTING RESPONSIBLY.
THIS POOR KID IS GONNA GET SOME HELP TONIGHT...

AT THE LIME-LIGHT NIGHTCLUB ON SIXTH AND TWENTIETH...
THE BASS IS UP ABOUT TEN LEVELS HIGHER THAN IT NEEDS TO BE.
FOR RICTOR AND SHATTERSTAR, THIS NIGHT OUT ON THE TOWN ELICITS COMPLETELY DIFFERENT RESPONSES.
'STAR, S'THIS GREAT OR WHAT?
OR WHAT.
THE SIGHTS AND SOUNDS-- A MIXTURE OF ENERGY AND CHAOS--
WHAT?!
EXACTLY.
WHAT'DJOU SAY?
NEVER MIND.
YOU GOTTA LOOSEN UP, MAN! LES' START PARTYIN'!!
I MIGHT, RICTOR, WERE IT NOT FOR THE FACT THIS PLACE REMINDS ME FAR TOO MUCH OF MY HOMEWORLD.
WHAT?
NOTHING.
THE EXTRA-DIMENSIONAL WARRIOR KNOWN ONLY AS SHATTERSTAR WATCHES HIS FRIEND SLIDE UP TO THE WOMEN AS IF BY SECOND NATURE.
AND STANDING IN THE MIDDLE OF THE MADNESS THESE YOUNG HUMANS CALL FUN-- HE WONDERS YET AGAIN--
--WHY CAN'T HE EVER FEEL AS IF HE FITS IN?

THE SONG HE KNOWS. HE'S SEEN IT ON THE TELEVISION--
-- THE BEASTIE BOYS-- SABO-TAGE.
IT'S A GOOD ONE. LOUD. PRIMITIVE.
CONFLICTED.
LIKE HE IS.
SHATTERSTAR LEFT HIS PLANET BECAUSE HE YEARNED FOR FREEDOM --
-- BUT HAVING FOUND THAT HERE ON EARTH, WHY DOES HE STILL FEEL LIKE A SLAVE ?
WHAT WILL IT TAKE TO MAKE HIM WHOLE?
WHOOPS-!
HEY, YOU SPILLED MY--
--WE DANCE. NOW.
BUT I DON'T--
NOW--OR I EAT YOU ALIVE RIGHT HERE IN FRONT OF EVERYONE!

MY NAME'S STECKY. WHAT'S YOURS?
SO, WHAT'S YOURS?
UHM... SHATTER--UHM... GAVEEDRA. THAT IS MY NAME.
THERE IS NO NEED TO SHOUT. I CAN HEAR YOU CLEARLY.
GO FOR IT, DUDE! ANDALE AHORA!
COOL. YOU GOT AN ACCENT. WHERE'RE YOU FROM?
UH... THAT WOULD BE... UHM... YOUR HAND... UH... HARD... TO EXPLAIN...
... EXCUSE ME, MISS, BUT I HAVE TO LEAVE NOW!
EXIT
HEY!!
'STAR--?
WHAT WILL IT TAKE TO MAKE THIS LONELY YOUNG MAN COME ALIVE FOR THE FIRST TIME IN HIS LIFE?

MEANWHILE, IN ISRAEL'S NEGEV DESERT...
...X-FORCE LEADERS CABLE AND DOMINO HAVE JOINED THE X-MEN AT THE REQUEST OF CHARLES XAVIER--
--A MAN WHO DOES NOT MAKE REQUESTS OFTEN... AND IS NOT OFTEN DENIED.*
*SEE CURRENT ISSUES OF UNCANNY X-MEN AND X-MEN.--BOB
THINGS HERE ARE A LITTLE MORE COMPLICATED THAN I EXPECTED, SAM.
AH DON'T KNOW IF YOU GET JUST WHAT AH'M SAYIN', SIR--
--WE FOUND BOBBY!
I REALLY DON'T THINK I CAN SEND DOM BACK WITH THE PACRAT* RIGHT NOW.
*PERSONNEL ASSAULT CARRIER FOR RECON/AQUATIC/ TERRAIN.--FOR YOUR INFORMATION BOB
I DO HEAR YOU, SAM, AND I'M SORRY, BUT THE SITUATION HERE REQUIRES OUR PRESENCE--
--BECAUSE WITHOUT US, THE WORLD AS WE KNOW IT MIGHT BE ENDING!

WHAT GOOD WOULD IT DO TO RESCUE DACOSTA IF THERE'S NOTHING LEFT TO BRING HIM HOME TO?
THINGS'RE THAT BAD?
PROBABLY WORSE THAN THAT, I'M AFRAID.
FINE. OKAY.
AH KNOW YOU WELL ENOUGH TO KNOW YOU DON'T CRY WOLF...
...WE'LL FIGURE OUT A WAY TA GET TO THE NORTH ATLANTIC.
AH'LL PUT A CALL IN TO MOIRA MACTAGGERT. MAYBE FORGE.
IF THE SITUATION HERE IMPROVES, SAM, WE'LL COME BACK AS--
SHKRKKZZKK
CABLE--?!
JKCHEEEEEEE
WE LOST 'IM?
FACHOOM
BRRMMMMM
SAM--?!
NO PROB, TER. AH PROTECTED MYSELF WITH A BLAST FIELD.
BUT AH'D LOVE TA KNOW WHY THE SYSTEMS JUST UP AN' EXPLODED ON--
THAT NOISE SOUNDS REALLY FAMILIAR, DOESN'T IT, GANG?

EEEEE
FIGHTING THE MLF ON THE ISLAND IN BERMUDA, WHEN DACOSTA DISAPPEARED ALONG WITH THAT TIME-HOPPIN' FREAK CALLED--
--VOLUS!
YOU'RE RIGHT, JIMMY! AN' I'LL NEVER FORGET THE LAST TIME WE HEARD IT!
X-FORCE?!
OH, GREAT! GONE FOR AS LONG AS I WAS AND LOOK WHERE I END UP!
NOT THAT I'M COMPLAINING, MIND YOU, BOYS AND GIRLS, BEGGARS CAN'T BE CHOOSERS, Y'KNOW--
--BUT EVER SINCE DACOSTA ABANDONED ME, I'VE HAD NOTHING BUT A MAD ON FOR YOU DUDES!
WHAT'D YOU SAY? ABANDONED YOU?
WHAT HAPPENED? WHERE'VE YOU AN' BOBBY BEEN FOR THE LAST SIX MONTHS?
ONLY SIX MONTHS WE BEEN GONE? FEKT, DON'T TIME FLY WHEN YOU'RE OUT OF TIME?
TALK ENGLISH, LOCUS!
ENGLISH? SURE, IF YOU WANNA BE DULL ABOUT IT.
HOW ABOUT D'BARIAN? OR BETTER YET, SHI'AR?
HJKTTEL FATH'EECH. CHALELL FOMAHTT, ARRIFFELL.

GIRL, YOU'RE ACTIN' FOUR SCOOPS SHORT OF AN ICE CREAM CONE.
WHAT'RE YOU DOIN' NOW?
MY TELEPORTATION PASSAGES ALWAYS HAVE A WAY OF SCREWING UP COMM-SYSTEMS FOR A DAY OR TWO--
--UNLESS I USE MY OWN ELECTRO-MAGNETIC FIELD FLEX TO REALIGN THE ARRAY.
IF I'M BACK HERE, THAT MEANS 'BERTO IS TOO. I NEED TO CONFIRM THAT.
WE CAN DO THAT FOR YOU. FIVE MINUTES BEFORE YOU SHOWED UP, WE FOUND OUT THAT HE'D BEEN--ON EARTH--ALL ALONG.
YEAH, SO YOU THINK.
YOU GOT A LOCATION-LOCK? GREAT. WE HAVE TO STOP HIM NOW, FUNKADRONES! BEFORE IT'S TOO LATE!
TOO LATE FOR WHAT?
CAN WE REWIND AND PLAY BACK THE LAST FEW MINUTES ON THIRTY-THREE RPM'S, PLEASE?
EEEEE
OH, WAY COOL! A REFERENCE TO RECORD ALBUMS!
YOU GOT NO IDEA HOW BUMMED OUT I WAS WHEN I FOUND OUT CD'S HAD BECOME OB-SOLETE BY THE TURN OF THE CENTURY!
TRUTH TO TELL, PRIDEWALKER, WE ACTUALLY DON'T HAVE THE TIME TO SPARE.
WHAT DID YOU CALL ME?
WAIT ONE MINUTE, GIRL! WE CAN'T JUST LET YOU UP AN' TAKE US--
THRIPP

RAIN HITS THE STREETS OF GREENWICH VILLAGE.
BUT LIKE SO MANY OTHER THINGS IN HER DIFFICULT LIFE--
--A SAFE HAVEN IS HARD TO FIND...
THE YOUNG GIRL NAMED PRISCILLA COLE TRIES TO FIND SHELTER FROM THE COMING STORM.
MEEEOWWRRR
GOT NOTHIN' FOR YOU, KITTY-CAT... I'M SORRY...
YEAH, BETTER RUN, YOU TRASH!
STAY AWAY FROM THE HOMES OF DECENT PEOPLE!
HEY YOU--!
WELCOME
WHERE DOES SHE RUN TO NOW? NO-WHERE.
WHO CAN SHE TURN TO FOR HELP? NO ONE.
IT'S ALL A MATTER OF LEARNING HOW TO HIT THEM.
BOOMER EASILY KEEPS PACE WITH THE GIRL.
HUH--? WHAT? LEAVE ME ALONE, GIRL.
WHO WOULD HAVE EVER EXPECTED HER TO BE IN THE EXCELLENT PHYSICAL CONDITION SHE'S NOW IN?
IN THIS LIFE, PRISCILLA'S LEARNED, NOBODY CARES.
LIFE, BOOMER'S LEARNED, HAS A HABIT OF THROWING CURVE-BALLS.
YOU KNOW THE RUNNING HAS TO STOP EVENTUALLY, DON'T YOU?

MY NAME IS TABITHA.
I'D LIKE TO HELP...IF YOU'LL LET ME.
THE CARD? YOU WORK FOR CHILD-WATCH?
NO. BUT I THINK THEY'RE WHAT YOU NEED RIGHT NOW.
YOU GOT NO IDEA WHAT I NEED, TAB.
YOU'D BE SURPRISED. I'VE BEEN THERE MY-SELF.
I THINK IF YOU JUST--
UGKCHEEE
--OH NO... NOT NOW...
AAAH, THE VILLAGE! JUST LIKE IT USED TO BE!
WISH WE COULD STOP N' SHOP.
HMM... THE ANTIQUE BOUTIQUES JUST A FEW BLOCKS AWAY...
DON'T ASK, BOOMER. PLEASE.
WAIT-- DON'T LEAVE!
HEY TAB, SAYIN' WE GOT SOMETHIN' GOIN' DOWN WOULD BE AN UNDER-STATEMENT.
I DON'T CARE ABOUT THAT, SAM! THAT GIRL NEEDS SOME HELP TONIGHT!
WE FOUND BOBBY! SEEMS THAT HELPED LOCUS COME BACK TO OUR TIME.
SHE SAYS WE HAVE TO GET TO HIM BEFORE HE MAKES SOME SORT OF TERRIBLE MISTAKE.
SIGH
GREAT. SOME CHOICE. SAVE OUR FRIEND OR SAVE ONE LOST LITTLE GIRL.
OKAY. I KNOW WHERE RIC AND SHATTYBUNS WENT.
LET'S GO GET THEM.

A FEW BLOCKS AWAY...
I DON'T THINK YOU WOULD UNDER-STAND.
TRY ME.
ALL RIGHT.
I HAVE NEVER BEEN WITH SOME-ONE... LIKE THAT... IN THAT WAY.
I HAVE NEVER--
LIVE JAZZ
THERE SOMETHIN' YOU WANNA TALK ABOUT, 'STAR?
'STAR, THAT AIN'T NOTHIN' TO BE ASHAMED OF, DUDE.
I MEAN, I TALK A GOOD GAME...
...BUT I NEVER HIT A HOME RUN EITHER.
NO... I AM NOT MAKING MYSELF CLEAR...
NEW YORK TIMES
SPORTS
...UNTIL TONIGHT, I HAD NEVER EVEN FELT SUCH STIRRINGS WITH-IN ME.
KRAKK
OH.
LISTEN, YOU'RE NOT FROM THIS PLANET--SO MAYBE, Y'KNOW--THAT'S NORMAL.
ARE YOU--I MEAN--DO YOU--HAVE--WHAT IT TAKES?
I WAS BIO-ENGINEERED TO FULLY SIMULATE PHYSICAL HUMAN INTERACTION.
BUT NO ONE EVER BOTHERED TO INSTILL THE EMOTIONAL RE-QUIREMENTS WHICH I HAVE LEARNED ARE ATTACHED TO SUCH ACTIONS.

OKAY, THAT'S COOL.
WE'LL WORK IT OUT TOGETHER.
I MEAN, IT'S ALL SOCIAL STUFF, RIGHT? YOU CAN LEARN THAT.
YOU HEAR SOMETHIN'?
IT IS FAMILIAR.
AND IT IS TROUBLE.
AND I AM WITHOUT WEAPONS.
DUDE, YOU ARE A WEAPON.
JGKCHEEEEEEEE
CATCH, GUYS!
PROUDSTAR? WHAT'S GOIN' DOWN?
TELL YOU ON THE WAY.
STEP INSIDE, IT'S AN INTERESTING TRIP.
'STAR, YOU GONNA BE OKAY WITH TONIGHT-- THE GIRL--AND OUR TALK, I MEAN?
"OKAY?"
OF COURSE I WILL BE, RICTOR.
WHAT OTHER CHOICE DO I HAVE?
NOW COME. OUR FRIENDS HAVE NEED OF US.
THRIPP

THE NORTH ATLANTIC...
SCREAMS CUT ACROSS THE DESOLATE LAND-SCAPE OF THE ANI-MUTATE ISLAND.
USUALLY THE CHATTERING OF THE GENETICALLY-TRANSFORMED ANIMALS WHO LIVE HERE DOMINATES THE STILL COLD AIR.
THIS NIGHT...
...THE SOUNDS HEARD ARE MOST DEFINITELY HUMAN...
...OR PERHAPS MORE ACCURATELY--
--INHUMAN!!
WILDSIDE'S DOWN!!
MOVE IT, DANI! MOVE IT!!
MIKE-- BEHIND YOU--!
FASHASH!!
DANIELLE MOONSTAR CAN ONLY WATCH IN HORROR AS FOREARM IS HIT BY THE BLACKENED FLASH OF SOLAR ENERGY.
HE WAS THE ONLY MEMBER OF THE MUTANT LIBERATION FRONT SHE FELT COMFORTABLE CALLING A FRIEND.
AND NOW SHE HAS TO ABANDON HIM...

...LEAVING HIM FACE DOWN ON THE ROCKY SHOAL, WITHOUT A CLUE AS TO WHETHER HE IS DEAD OR ALIVE.
A REFLECTION OF THE CONSTANT STRUGGLE SHE HAS FACED SINCE JOINING THIS TERRORIST ORGANIZATION IN ORDER TO BETRAY THEM.
SHOULD THE LIVES OF THE FEW BE SACRIFICED IF IT SAVES THE LIVES OF THE MANY?
THE ANSWER, ACCORDING TO REIGNFIRE, IS "YES."
AND HE HAS PROVEN HIMSELF A FIRM BELIEVER IN PRACTICING WHAT HE PREACHES!
FASHASH!
DARKWIND! IF I CAN JUST GET TO HIM IN TIME--
NO. BY THE GREAT BEAR, NO--!
SHREKTH

DARKWIND-- MY HORSE--! YOU KILLED HIM--?
OH, SWEET SPIRIT, THERE'S NOTHING LEFT OF YOU, IS THERE?
IT'S HOPELESS...
... I CAN'T DEFEAT YOU ALONE...
DANI, GIRL... THAT'S ALWAYS BEEN YOUR MISTAKE...
... YOU'VE NEVER BEEN ALONE.
SAM--?
X-FORCE?
LOCUS--?! BUT HOW--?!
WE'LL FILL YOU IN SOON AS WE TAKE OUT TH' TRASH.
REIGNFIRE-- WE WANNA KNOW WHAT YOU'VE DONE WITH ROBERTO DACOSTA!!

YOUR NAIVE CHARM WORE OUT ITS WELCOME WITH ME QUITE A LONG TIME AGO, SAM.
THE ANSWER TO WHERE BOBBY DACOSTA HAS BEEN SINCE HE DISAPPEARED MONTHS AGO--
--SHOULD HAVE BEEN QUITE CLEAR TO YOU--
--HAD YOU BEEN CAPABLE OF ACCEPTING THE OBVIOUS.
STOP TALKIN' IN RIDDLES, REIGNFIRE!
SAM, YOU DON'T UNDER-STAND--
NO, DANI, HE DOESN'T.
BUT PERHAPS THIS WILL SHED THE DARK LIGHT OF TRUTH ON THINGS...
DEAR LORD, NO.

GOD WAS NOT INVOLVED IN WHAT I HAVE BEEN FORCED TO DO--
--OR THE REASONS WHY I HAVE UNDER-TAKEN THE MISERABLE TASK OF SETTING THIS PLANET RIGHT.
IT IS ME.
REIGNFIRE IS AND HAS ALWAYS BEEN ROBERTO DACOSTA.
BUT IT CAN'T BE-- I MEAN, SUNSPOT WAS WITH US ON THE MISSION WHERE WE FOUGHT YOU!
BOBBY-- HOW-- WHY?!
AH, BUT TIME HAS A HABIT OF PULLING THE RUG OUT--
--FROM UNDER THE FEET OF ANYONE WEARING AN "X" ON THEIR BELT, DOESN'T IT?
BECAUSE, SAM, THINGS CAN'T CON-TINUE GOING THE WAY THEY HAVE.
THE WORLD IS COMING TO AN END, SOON, OLD FRIEND--

--AND I REFUSE TO SIMPLY STAND BY AND--
--WATCH--
KRYEEEEK
--IT--
--HAPPEN--?
WHAT'S GOING ON HERE? WHAT KIND OF A TRICK IS THIS--
KRYEEEK

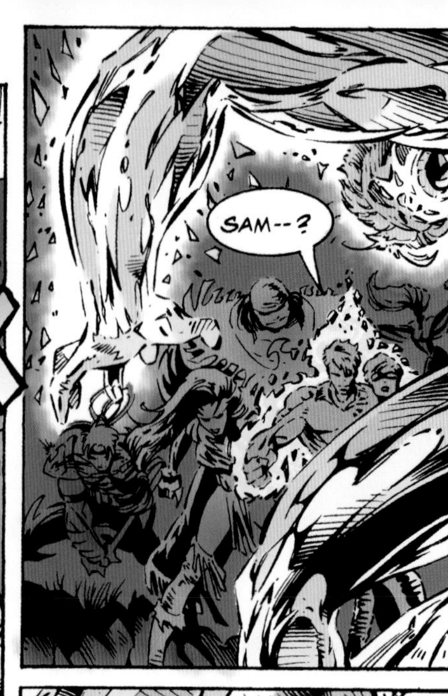

X-Men trading-card art by Larry Stroman, Peter Scanlan & Tom Fleming

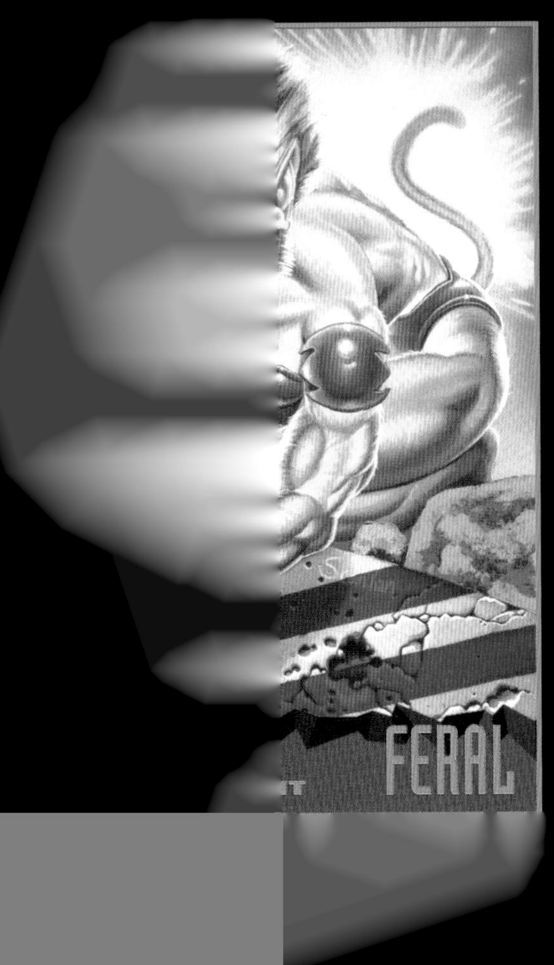

1995 Fleer Ultra X-Men trading-card art by Dimitri Patelis, Joann Daley & Luis Perez

1995 Fleer Ultra X-Men trading-card art by Robert Mitz, Alfons Kiefer & Joann Daley

Marvel Swimsuit Special #3 (1994) pinup by Bret Blevins & Tom Smith

If there is anyone who likes a good time, it is definitely **Boomer** of the radical mutant X-Force. Of course, the definition of a good time tends to vary according to one's point of view—which could explain the smiles on Gorgon and his fellow Inhumans, as well as the energy "time bomb" heading their way.

Marvel Swimsuit Special #3 (1994) pinup by Salvador Larroca, Sergio Melia & Tom Smith

Many humans consider karaoke an evil, annoying pastime. Many do not. But when sonic mutants Banshee and his daughter Siryn perform a duet, the opinion of the occasion would seem to be unanimous and unequivocal. Though it is not my place to evaluate, I am gladdened at this time to be the Watcher...and not the listener.
SALVADOR
SERGIO
+ SMITH
94

Marvel® Comics
Book X-FORCE
38
Story Page 33
Line-Up Page #42
OCH -- SAM! 'TIS AMAZIN'!
GLORIOUS! THE WAY THAT HE SEES THE WORLD.
NOT FOR THE BETTER, NOR THE WORSE -- JUST SO DIFFERENT!
EVEN THOUGH YOU SEEM T'BE ALL RIGHT, RAHNE, AH'M STILL NOT TOO SURE ABOUT ALL THIS.
AH WISH AH KNEW WHAT T'DO. AH WISH AH HAD YOUR TRUST, GIRL.
MY EXISTENCE OBVIOUSLY CAUSES YOU GREAT PAIN, CANNONBALL. FOR THIS, I APOLOGIZE. BUT I CANNOT CHANGE WHO I AM NOR WHAT I LOOK LIKE... TO MAKE YOUR LIFE EASIER.
I DO NOT TRULY UNDER-STAND MY ORIGINS, NOR THE ORIGINS OF THE PHALANX. THERE IS MUCH WE MUST ALL LEARN--
--BUT IT IS CLEAR THAT NEITHER MAN NOR MUTANTKIND SHOULD SUFFER SIMPLY BECAUSE MY RACE EXISTS.
WE ALL HAVE VARIED REASONS FOR BEING HERE, SAMUEL--
--BUT THE ONLY WAY WE WILL ACCOMPLISH THESE DISPARATE GOALS--
--IS BY ATTEMPTING TO INFILTRATE THE BABEL SPIRE.
IN SHORT, IF WE ARE TO SUCCEED, YOU MUST PUT ASIDE YOUR FEAR, YOUR PREJUDICE OF ME--
--AND YOU MUST FIND THAT TRUST.
42

Character sketches by Joe Madureira

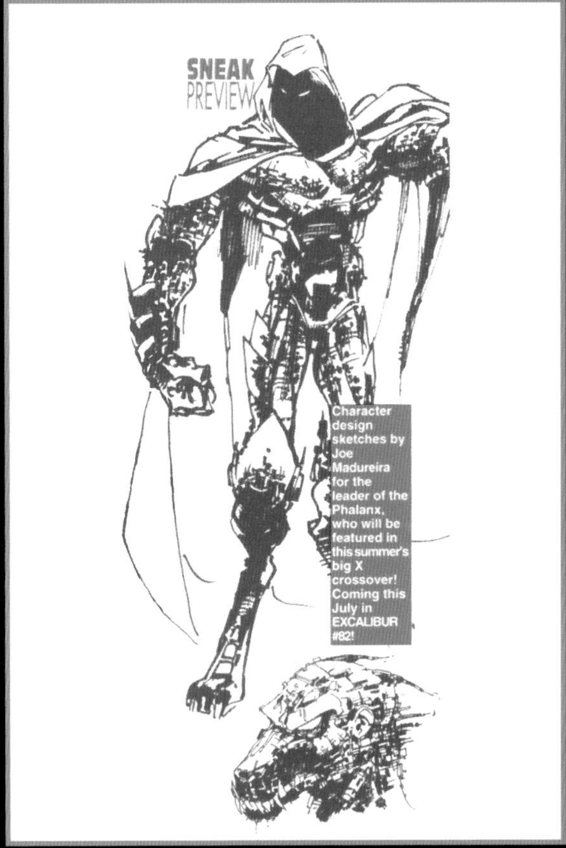

SNEAK
PREVIEW
Character design sketches by Joe Madureira for the leader of the Phalanx, who will be featured in this summer's big X crossover! Coming this July in EXCALIBUR #82!

The non-deluxe editions of each "Phalanx Covenant" crossover issue replaced the metallic foil stripe with a red stripe.

MARVEL COMICS

$2.00 US
$2.70 CAN
38
SEP
UK £1.25

X-FORCE

PHALANX COVENANT

LIFE SIGNS
PART 2

MARVEL COMICS

$2.50 US
$3.40 CAN
82
OCT

EXCALIBUR

PHALANX COVENANT

LIFE SIGNS
PART 3